The Great Walls

Exploring the City's Ancient Defences

Ken Smith

Tom Yellowley

Tyne Bridge Publishing

Acknowledgements

The authors and Tyne Bridge Publishing wish to thank the following for their kind help and advice in the preparation of this book: Ian Ayris; Roger Fern; David Heslop; Paul Macdonald; Alan Morgan; Barry Redfern; Northumberland & Newcastle Society; the staff of Newcastle City Library Heritage Section; Tyne & Wear Specialist Conservation Team.

Illustrations

Map of the Town Walls, inside front cover, by 1f Design.
Map of the Town Walls, inside back cover, from Isaac Thompson's map of Newcastle in 1746.

Photography ©Tom Yellowley unless otherwise indicated.

Archive illustrations are from the collections at Newcastle Libraries unless otherwise indicated. Drawings by Robert Bertram (pages 42 and 75) first appeared in The *Walls of Newcastle upon Tyne*, Northumberland & Newcastle Society, 1951.

Front cover: Heber Tower in use as a Blacksmith's shop in 1903.
Back cover: The Castle Keep from Castle Stairs, Tom Yellowley.
Opposite: All Saints Church from Corner Turret, Anna Flowers.
Title page: Roman stones on the West Road, Anthony Flowers

©Ken Smith, Tom Yellowley, 2012
Published by
City of Newcastle upon Tyne
Newcastle Libraries & Information Service
Tyne Bridge Publishing, 2012

www.tynebridgepublishing.co.uk
www.newcastle.gov.uk/libraries

ISBN: 978-1-85795-209-4

All rights reserved. No part of this book may be reproduced, stored or introduced into a retrieval system or transmitted in any way or by any means (electronic, mechanical, photocopying, recording or otherwise) without the prior permission of the publishers.

Printed in the UK.

Contents

	page
The Great Walls: an introduction	5
On the Roman Frontier	6
Hadrian's Legacy	9
In Defence of the Town	15
A Tour of the Walls	23
The Mystery Wall	70
Newcastle's Civil War Siege	72
Geordies and Jacobites	81
The New Castle	84

West Walls and back Stowell Street around 1880. In the distance, far right, a windmill minus sails, on Darn Crook, can just be made out. We are looking towards Morden Tower, which at that time was a dwelling. Morden Tower is now well known as a venue for poetry readings.

The Great Walls of Newcastle

Newcastle's heritage is a source of great pride to the people of Tyneside; it is a fundamental part of the city's identity and distinctiveness. The international significance of Hadrian's Wall is recognised in its World Heritage Site status, its majestic size and length enjoyed and celebrated by thousands of visitors. That Newcastle's medieval defences once had equally impeccable credentials is perhaps less well known. 'The walls here of Newcastle' wrote the 17th century traveller John Lithgow, 'are a great deal stronger than those of York, and not unlike to the walls of Avignon, but especially of Jerusalem.'

Even today the city's Castle Keep is recognised as perhaps the finest Norman Keep in England and the remains of the Town Walls are regarded by the architectural historian Sir Nikolaus Pevsner as amongst the five finest surviving medieval walls in the country. Almost two thousand years of history live in the three heritage assets which form the core of this book – the Roman Wall, Newcastle Castle and the medieval Town Walls. 'Walls have tongues' wrote Jonathan Swift – these walls tell a fascinating story.

In time the walls which were a barrier to the town's enemies would become a barrier to its growth and prosperity. Where many of our 18th and 19th century forefathers saw these ancient structures as a hindrance to be swept away to allow the town to expand, we see them as treasured parts of our historic city. They remain an active part of modern life (the poets in the Morden Tower, the walkers along the Roman wall and the visitors to the Castle Keep bring different uses to those the builders intended). Most

importantly they are portals to our past.

Preserving, managing and interpreting them for our own and future generations is essential if we are to understand, enjoy and learn from them.

This duty of care includes the continuing archaeological search for hidden remains of Hadrian's Wall, conserving the fabric of our medieval monuments, making these historic places accessible and interpreting the past through new media.

From plaques to panels to digital devices, the ways in which we can tell the stories of the city grow as quickly as the technology itself expands. Bringing the Black Gate back to life as the heart of Old Newcastle provides a focus for the future telling of the city's past. Understanding our historic environment is the bedrock upon which we build the desire to preserve and enjoy the past. *The Great Walls of Newcastle* adds greatly to our knowledge, appreciation and pride in this great city.

Ian Ayris, Team Manager,
Urban Design and Conservation Team,
Newcastle City Council, 2012

The Riverside Tower, where the Town Wall met the natural defence of the Tyne, is excavated, 1988. Its outline is now picked out at the entrance to the Copthorne Hotel which is on the site of the tower.

On the Roman Frontier

In 122 AD, the Emperor Hadrian ordered a defensive frontier barrier to be constructed from east to west across what is now the far north of England. It was said that the aim of this great barrier was to separate the lands under complete Roman control to the south from the territory of the non-Roman tribes – the so-called barbarians – to the north, an area that corresponds to present day Scotland, an extensive part of Northumberland and a smaller section of Cumbria.

There is uncertainty among archaeologists and historians as to the extent to which the wall was under attack from the north. However, the barrier was probably intended to act as a deterrent to would-be enemies rather than an impregnable defensive line.

When completed, Hadrian's Wall ran for 73 miles (80 Roman miles) from Wallsend on the River Tyne to Bowness-on-Solway. It was originally intended that this long 'screen' should extend from what is now Newcastle to Bowness. During construction the scheme was extended for three miles eastwards, ending at Segedunum (now Wallsend).

At first, Hadrian's Wall – or the Roman Wall as it is frequently called – was built in stone from Wallsend to the River Irthing at Gilsland. From this point onwards, westwards to Bowness, it was made of turf. Later the turf would be replaced with stone.

At some point during construction it was also decided that the width of the barrier should be reduced, resulting in the 'narrow' and 'broad' sections of wall.

Forts with barracks for soldiers were constructed at intervals along the length of the frontier. Between them, generally at intervals of one Roman mile (1,480 metres), fortified gatehouses – today known as milecastles – were built. Two turrets were placed between each two milecastles to act as look-out posts.

Immediately to the north of the wall there was a defensive ditch and mound except in places where steep cliffs or other features provided a natural defence. Running along the southern side was a narrow military zone that was eventually provided with a road – known as the Military Way – linking the various forts, milecastles and turrets. This was bounded to the south by another large defensive ditch with earthwork mounds on each side. The three features were collectively known as the vallum.

There has been some debate as to the height of the wall, but many now believe it was around 15ft. The 'broad' sections were 10ft wide and the 'narrow' generally 8ft.

A small fort was built in the late second or early third century to guard the Roman bridge across the Tyne at what would become Newcastle. The bridge was known as Pons Aelius (Aelius was the name of the Emperor Hadrian's family) and the fort took its name from the bridge.

Coin from the reign of the Emperor Hadrian.

Several sections of Hadrian's Wall survive within Newcastle on its western side. Strung out along the West Road, thousands of drivers pass them each day.

Today, Hadrian's Wall is a World Heritage Site, designated by Unesco, so, small as they are, Newcastle's sections of this ancient barrier are of major international importance.

Hadrian's Legacy

West and East along the line of the Wall

Westgate Road Milecastle

Near the foot of Westgate Hill, just west of its junction with Grainger Street, there was a milecastle, now hidden under and behind shops next to Newcastle Arts Centre on the south side of Westgate Road. The remains were found in 1985. A small section of the milecastle stones below an outdoor staircase can be seen in Black Swan Yard, behind Newcastle Arts Centre (right). The milecastle's front wall is buried beneath the pavement of Westgate Road.

Steve Brock

Tantalising traces of the Roman Wall to the east and the west of the city centre have been located, but the exact path of the central section has proved elusive because of centuries of building and rebuilding. Foundations have been uncovered at the bottom of Westgate Road, near the Literary and Philosophical Society, and to the east near City Road, and in other spots, but to see the wall itself we have to travel beyond the city centre.

Condercum Fort, Benwell, and a local god

Continuing west along the West Road (A186), at Benwell the remains of a Roman Fort, Condercum, are hidden beneath housing, a road and other modern developments. The fort straddled the wall and a small part of it lies under the West

9

Road. Most of the remains lie beneath homes immediately to the south. There is a smaller section to the north, with a reservoir overlying most of it. Condercum, like most Roman forts, contained barracks, a commanding officer's house, a headquarters building, workshops, granaries, stables and a hospital.

In Denhill Park there is a well-preserved vallum crossing, pictured above. The crossing is the only one on the wall now visible. This causeway of earth with stone sides provided access across the ditch to the fort. The stone foundations of an impressive gateway can be seen in the centre of the crossing. The vallum is also a prominent feature here. The remains of a bath house and traces of a civilian settlement have been found in the area outside the fort.

Only a short distance to the east of Condercum, in Broomridge Avenue, stand the remains of a Roman temple. It is dedicated to the god Antenociticus. There are no references to this god elsewhere, so he is likely to be a local deity.

The temple, pictured above, on a small plot between semi-detached homes, features two replica altars. The originals, together with the head from the statue of the god (pictured opposite), are in Newcastle's Great North Museum.

Denton Burn Walls

Further west along the West Road past Newcastle Crematorium, there are two remnants of the wall at Denton Burn. One of these, a very small area of stones, is at the side of a garage forecourt. This tiny portion reaches a height of three courses. The other, a larger and longer section, is a short distance to the west, next to the main road and close to Denton Burn library. These remains reach a maximum height of four courses.

Denton Hall Turret and Wall, and other remains

Beyond Denton Library is Denton Hall Turret – number 7B. The remains of the turret and an attached stretch of the broad wall can be seen beside the road. The stones reach a maximum height of six or seven courses and there is a stone platform inside. This was used as the base for a ladder to reach the upper storey (about 30ft high). The section of wall here is 213ft long and reaches a height of three courses in places.

Denton Hall Turret and wall.

The turret takes its name from the 17th century East Denton Hall, a short distance away on the other side of West Road at its junction with Newcastle's Western Bypass. Today the hall is the residence of the Roman Catholic Bishop of Hexham and Newcastle.

At South West Denton there is a stretch of wall next to the main road. It consists of two small sections and a much longer one. The longer portion has a maximum of three courses.

The remains of Milecastles 9 and 10 are further to the west near Chapel House and Walbottle Dene respectively. Of Milecastle 9, only a low area of stones is visible. The remains of a wall of Milecastle 10 are on land at Dene House, close to Walbottle Dene.

Discoveries at Byker

In 2000, redevelopment work in the Shields Road area of Byker in Newcastle's East End led to the discovery of the foundations of a stretch of the wall. Part of these remains is now visible in Hadrian Square at the side of Shiclds Road, close to the East End swimming pool.

Archaeologists also discovered three rows of pits in this area, between the wall foundations and the ditch to the north. Each is believed to have held wooden branches, with multiple sharpened forks, which were installed as a further barrier to defend the frontier from attack.

Top, *the three large stones in this photo from around 1880 were said to mark the line of the Roman Wall near Beckington Steam Mill, Ouseburn Valley. The stones were later moved to the quay wall.*

Above, *remains of the wall at Hadrian Square, Byker.*

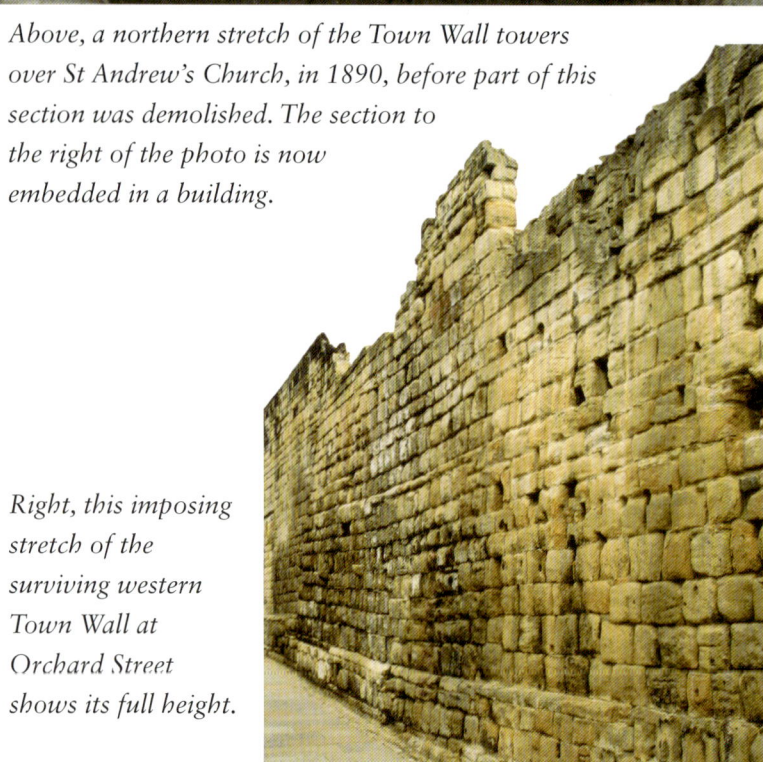

Above, a northern stretch of the Town Wall towers over St Andrew's Church, in 1890, before part of this section was demolished. The section to the right of the photo is now embedded in a building.

Right, this imposing stretch of the surviving western Town Wall at Orchard Street shows its full height.

In Defence of the Town

The medieval walls of Newcastle were built in the 13th and 14th centuries to defend the town against attack by invading Scots armies or other military threats. Newcastle was frequently the assembly point for English troops preparing for expeditions north of the border or to meet Scottish forces that had crossed into England and was therefore an important military town as well as a key port and burgeoning centre of trade, mainly leather and wool at that time. Coal would become a major export by the 16th century.

In 1265, during the reign of Henry III, a wall tax, known as 'murage', was imposed on townsmen for constructing this barrier, although it is thought that work on the walls did not start until a few years later, probably during the reign of Edward I, which began in 1272.

The work was largely paid for by local taxation and some of the towers and gates were financed by the town's monasteries, wealthy merchants and nobles who owned property in the town.

One story claims that a wealthy townsman was taken prisoner by the Scots during the reign of Edward I and 'being at last ransomed by a large sum, he, first of all, began to surround the town with walls'. There is no proof that this is true, but perhaps this particular townsman boosted the money already collected through tax and enabled the work to be started.

The walls took many years to build, but were largely complete by the middle of the 14th century. The Quayside section is believed to have been finished a little later.

The map of 1746, inside the back cover of this book, shows the shape and extent of the completed Town Walls.

Antiquarian John Leland, writing of Newcastle in the 16th century, declared: 'The strength and magnificence of the walling of this town far passeth all the walls of the cities of England, and most of the towns of Europe.'

Back Stowell Street in the 1930s, drawn by Byron Dawson. The walkway along the top of the wall, and a turret, are clearly depicted.

The walls, a little over two miles long and built from locally quarried sandstone, featured a walkway along the top, fortified gates, seventeen towers and a series of turrets. The dimensions of this impressive barrier varied, generally ranging from 20ft to 30ft high and 7ft to 10ft thick.

Immediately inside the walls an access street ran around most or perhaps all of the circuit. This narrow passage can still be seen behind Stowell Street and Bath Lane. Pink Lane forms another part of this passage, although it has lost its section of wall.

The towers were semi-circular on their outward-facing sides and squared off on their town-facing sides, taking the form of a letter D. Loopholes were provided in the towers for arrows. Examples can still be seen on the West Walls.

The rectangular turrets in between the towers were essentially observation posts, but they too featured loopholes for use by archers. The turrets were flush with the outward face of the walls but projected on stone corbles to the rear. There were statues of armed warriors or knights positioned on the turret tops.

The main fortified gates were the key entry points to the town and were kept locked at night. The West Gate and New Gate were the most heavily fortified.

The other main entrances were the Pilgrim Street Gate, Pandon Gate, Sand Gate, Bridge End Gate and Close Gate. The Bridge End Gate was at the northern end of the Tyne Bridge, completed around 1250, well before work on the walls was started.

There were a number of 'water' gates leading to the Tyne quayside and several postern (private) gates, which in wartime would serve as 'sally-ports' from which defenders could 'sally forth' to carry out raids against forces besieging the town.

To stand any chance of repulsing an attack, good

The inside passage of the West Walls in 1786.

organisation was clearly needed. Accordingly, Newcastle was divided into twenty-four wards (districts) and the residents of each ward were responsible for the defence of a particular gate or tower. Records tell us that in 1402 a hundred men kept watch on the walls 'at the charge [expense] of the inhabitants'.

As the need for the walls to defend the town lessened, the towers became meeting places for the Newcastle craft and trade guilds (companies) from the 17th to the 19th centuries. They were leased out by the town corporation. In some cases the guilds carried out alterations and improvements to the buildings to make their gatherings more comfortable and to add an element of prestige to their organisations.

The guilds flourished during the Middle Ages and Tudor period. On the Feast of Corpus Christi they took part in a procession through the town and members performed plays with a religious theme.

Braveheart – the statue of William Wallace at Edinburgh Castle.

(Photo by Kjetil Bjornsrud.)

In 1297, Scots warrior William Wallace led a raid deep into Northumberland following his victory at Stirling Bridge, but he avoided attacking Newcastle after townsmen met him with a show of force. He and his men retreated northwards 'laden with spoils'.

In 1299, after the Scottish defeat at the Battle of Falkirk the previous year, Wallace led another incursion across the border.

According to historian Eneas Mackenzie (1827), despite the hammer blow of Falkirk, Wallace 'still maintained the contest for liberty' and 'led his chosen band to the walls of Newcastle, which he assailed in vain, being always repulsed by the valour of the inhabitants'. This implies that some

This 16th century print illustrating Newcastle's devastating fire of 1248, gives some impression of what the walls might have looked like. The walls were not in existence in 1248, but the artist may have based his imaginary view on what he could see in his own time.

sections of the walls were complete by 1299. When, in 1305, Wallace was hanged, drawn and quartered in London, his body was dismembered and sent to towns in England and Scotland. His right arm was exhibited on the bridge at Newcastle and other parts of his body made gruesome displays on Newcastle Keep.

Newcastle was besieged by the Scots twice during the 14th century, but both attacks were unsuccessful. In 1342, David II and his army crossed the border but were repulsed when they tried to capture the town. A party of 200 defenders sallied forth from a gate by night, surprising soldiers of the besieging Scottish army and taking the Earl of Murray prisoner in his tent. Afterwards, the Scots attacked the walls but came up against a strong defence led by the captain of the castle, Sir John Neville.

The second attack came in 1388 when the second Earl of Douglas and another Scottish force invaded England, raiding as far south as Durham. Afterwards they turned northwards and appeared before the walls of Newcastle. The Earl of Northumberland had sent his sons, Sir Henry and Sir Ralph Percy, and their army to Newcastle to reinforce the garrison and repulse the Scots.

Skirmishes developed between the town garrison and the Scottish force immediately outside the walls. During one of these encounters Sir Henry, better known to history as Harry Hotspur, was knocked from his horse by the Earl of Douglas who captured his opponent's pennon.

Douglas challenged Hotspur to take up the fight again at Otterburn in Northumberland and the Scots withdrew. A day or two later, Hotspur and Sir Ralph, accompanied by their men, left Newcastle in pursuit of Douglas. However, at Otterburn the Scots won the moonlight battle of Chevy Chase (Cheviot Forest) and Hotspur was taken prisoner. The Scots suffered a serious loss when Douglas was killed. The battle is remembered in the *Ballad of Chevy Chase*.

In 1644, during the Civil War, the town was again besieged, this time by a Scottish army numbering around 30,000. It was the last time the walls were attacked.

As the need for defensive walls grew less and their state deteriorated most sections of the wall were removed during the late 18th and into the 19th centuries. By this time they were regarded as a hindrance to business and traffic. However, several sections survived and are an important part of Newcastle's heritage.

Above, right, a map of 1610 (hand coloured in the 1880s) showing the town neatly surrounded by the walls.

Below, right, this map shows Newcastle in 1639 and indicates where the defensive guns were placed within the Town Walls at the start of the Civil War when Newcastle was threatened by the Scots.

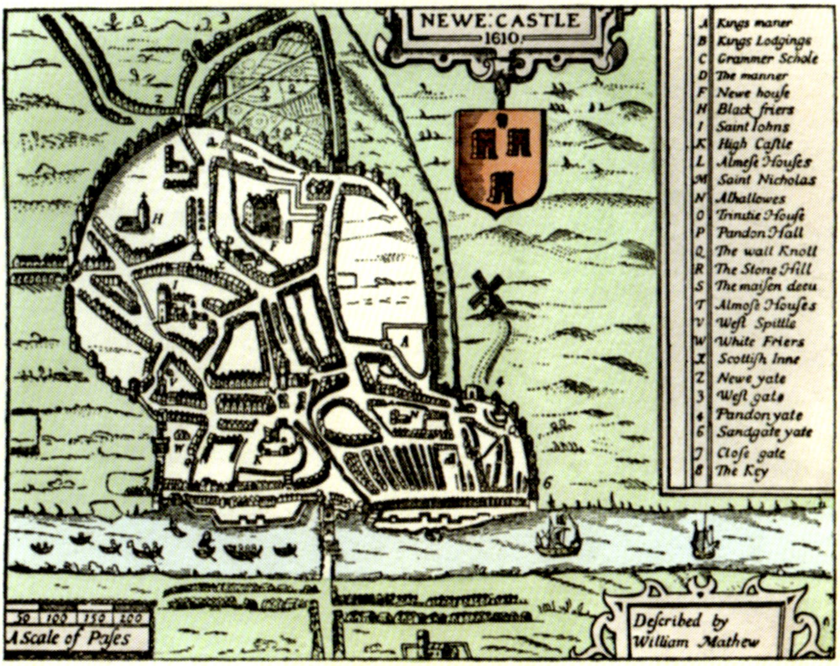
NEWE CASTLE 1610
A Kings maner
B Kings Lodgings
C Grammer Schole
D The manner
F Newe house
H Black friers
I Saint Iohns
K High Castle
L Almese Houses
M Saint Nicholas
N Alhallowes
O Trinitie House
P Pandon Hall
Q The wall Knoll
R The Stone Hill
S The maisen deeu
T Almose Houses
V West Spittle
W White Friers
X Scottish Inne
2 Newe yate
3 West gate
4 Pandon yate
6 Sandgate yate
7 Close gate
8 The Key
A Scale of Pases
Described by William Mathew

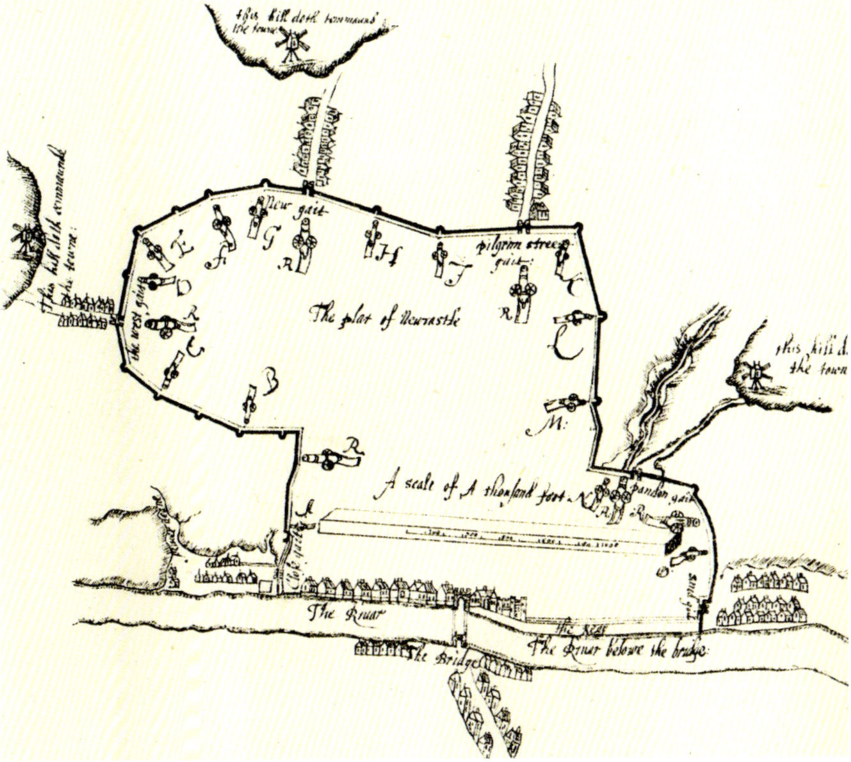
The plat of Newcastle
New gait
pilgrim stree gait
the west gait
Pandon gait
A scale of A thousand foot
The Riuar
The Bridge
The Riuar belowe the bridge

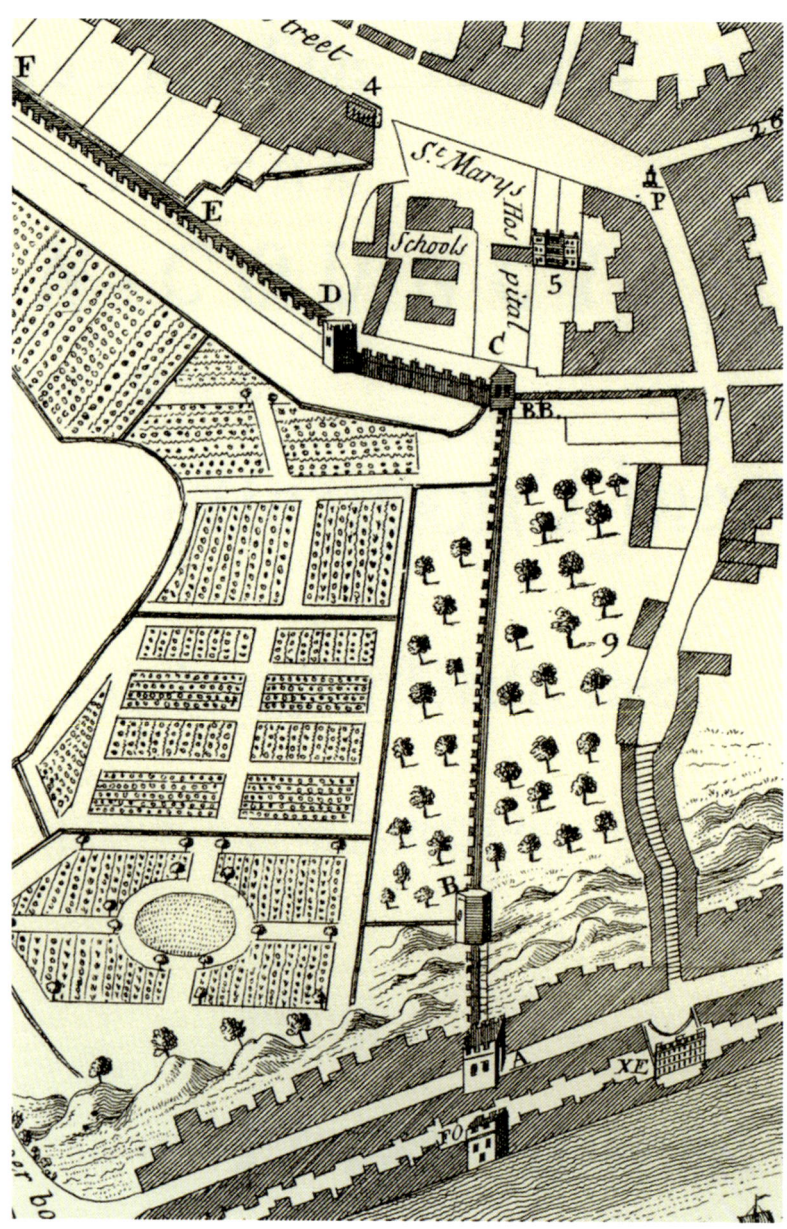

Henry Bourne's map of 1736 shows the Riverside Tower, Close Gate, and Whitefriar Tower as well as the steep stairs leading to The Close. Today, it is still just possible to imagine the edge of the town as it was then. Some of the old buildings on the Close, such as the Cooperage, preserve the medieval atmosphere. The orchards that give Orchard Street its name are clearly visible on the map.

A Tour of the Walls

Close Gate to West Gate

Today, the visitor to Newcastle can still trace the route of the Town Walls and tour the line of the surviving sections. There are information plaques along the route.

The Close Gate was on the south western side of the wall, and took its name from The Close, a major street running along the riverside from Sandhill. The site of the Close Gate is immediately outside the front of the Copthorne Hotel. The gate, described as narrow, awkward and dangerous, was demolished in 1797.

The Riverside Tower was to the south of this gate, by the banks of the Tyne. It became the meeting place of the Newcastle Carpenters' Company and was later used by the Sailmakers. The tower's outline is marked out in the floor of the entrance to the Copthorne Hotel.

Close Gate and the Close.

From the Close Gate the wall ran northwards steeply up the slopes of the Tyne Gorge. The wall-top walk at this point ascended in 140 steps to the Whitefriar Tower. It must have been a physically demanding stretch to patrol. Small wonder that the steps were called the 'breakneck' stairs. Some of the remains of these stairs and the wall, somewhat overgrown, are visible opposite the hotel. Today, a more recent stairway climbs the steep slope.

The Whitefriar Tower, which was at the top of the bank, was named after the adjoining house of the Carmelites or White Friars. It became the meeting place of the Masons Company and the Bricklayers, Plasterers and Meters (according to Mackenzie, the Meters or Metters exercised the exclusive privilege of measuring all corn imported or exported through Newcastle). In the late 18th century the building was converted into an ice house.

In their rules of 1445, the Bricklayers and Plasterers were required to 'play, at their own charge, two

Remains of the Town Wall by the stairs.

Whitefriar Tower, from the west, around 1825. In 1644, during the Civil War, a breach was made in the wall near here when the Scots stormed the town.

plays, viz.: *The Creation of Adam* and *The Flying of Our Lady into Egypt*'. Another regulation stated 'that if any free brother, or his wife, should die, all the lights of the fellowship should be borne before them…'

The early 1840s witnessed the demolition of the tower to make way for the building of Hanover Street, which led upwards to Hanover Square and gave access to the newly built Bonded Warehouses lining the street.

The steep area between The Close and Whitefriars Place at the top of the bank has been landscaped as 'hanging gardens'.

From the Whitefriar Tower the wall ran northwards along the eastern side of Orchard Street, where an impressively long high section survives (see photo on page 14), together with a shorter, but still high, section. The photograph, right, shows the thickness of the wall.

Orchard Street takes its name from the orchards that were cultivated on both sides of the wall here and were owned by the White Friars. For many years the wall in this area ran through the interior of a modern brewery. The demolition of the brewery in the late 20th century brought it back into public view.

Immediately north of this stretch, the wall disappears under the railway approaches to the Central Station.

Nearby Hanover Square was formerly part of the White Friars' grounds. Next to it is Clavering Place, which features two fine 18th century houses.

At the Denton or Neville Tower, the wall turned sharply westwards towards the West Gate. The site of the tower is now covered by rail tracks close to the Central Station.

The Denton or Neville Tower is said to have been named after John de Denton, a bailiff of Newcastle in 1339, or some

25

of his family, and after the Nevilles, a prominent family whose nearby house, Westmoreland Place, was roughly where the North of England Mining Institute headquarters and Newcastle Literary and Philosophical Society library now stand. The tower was used as the meeting place for the Wallers, Bricklayers and Plasterers – the Bricklayers and Plasterers had moved there from the Whitefriar Tower in around 1711.

Henry Bourne, the 18th century Newcastle historian, suggested that the postern below the Denton or Neville Tower was made so that the White Friars could have access to the public open space known as The Forth and neighbouring fields.

He also believed that it was possibly from the White Friars' postern, during the siege of 1342, that 200 townsmen sallied out and took the Earl of Murray prisoner in his tent.

The White Friars' postern was remarkably strong, with gates of oak, iron doors and a heavy portcullis. The arms of the Clavering and Shaftoe families were cut in stone above the gateway.

The West Spital, Stank, Gunner and Pink towers all stood between the Neville or Denton Tower and the West Gate.

The West Spital Tower took its name from the medieval Hospital of St Mary the Virgin, which was in the area between the Royal Station Hotel and Union Rooms, at the junction of Westgate Road and Neville Street. In those days a 'hospital' offered lodgings and food to travellers such as pilgrims, and gave help to the poor and sick. In 1290 the master and brethren of the hospital obtained a patent for installing their own postern gate in the walls.

In 1862, the statue of steam locomotive pioneer George Stephenson (1781-1848) was erected in the area where the hospital stood. Born at Wylam, a few miles to the west of Newcastle, Stephenson honed the steam locomotive into a workable means of transport, engineered several important early railways and invented a safety lamp for miners known appropriately as the 'Geordie.'

In 1823, George and his son, Robert, founded the first

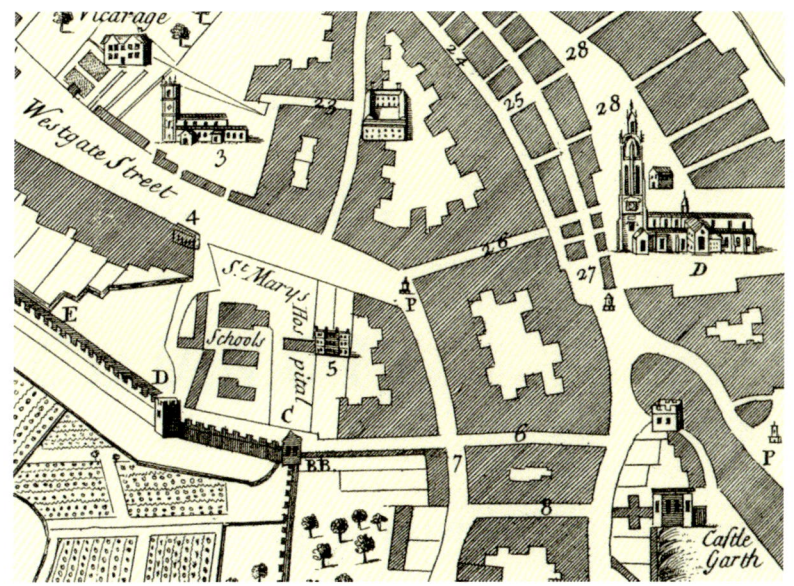

Bourne's 1736 map, above, shows St Mary's Hospital, the Denton Tower (C), approximately where the Mining Institute and Literary and Philosophical Society are now, and the West Spital Tower (D), not far from George Stephenson's statue. The sites of the towers are both now beneath the Central Station.

The St Mary's Hospital area from Westgate Road around 1863. The large building is the Lit and Phil. In front is Westmoreland Place, home of the Neville family. The Mining Institute occupies that spot now. The Stephenson monument is right.

purpose built railway locomotive factory in the world in South Street, behind Newcastle's Central Station. Robert designed the magnificent High Level Bridge, which spans the Tyne only a short distance away.

The West Spital Tower was almost certainly built by the master and brethren of the Hospital of St Mary the Virgin for their security and defence. Its site is today beneath the Central Station near the eastern end of the railway platforms.

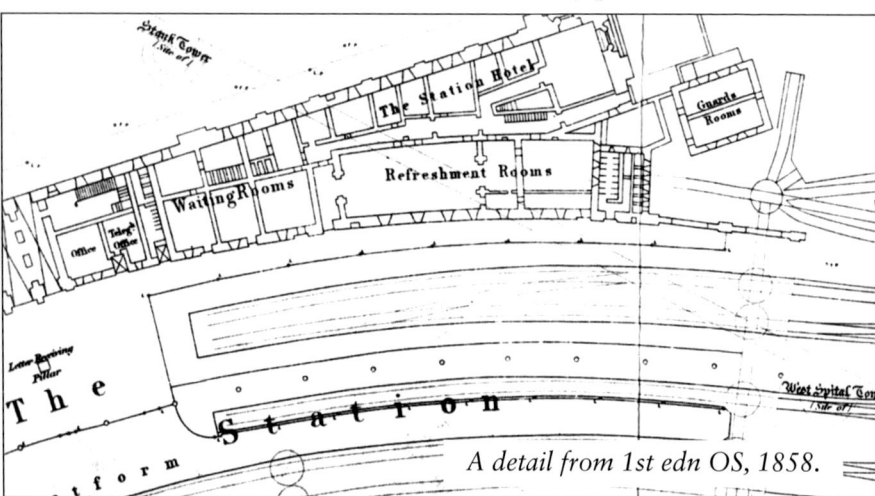

A detail from 1st edn OS, 1858.

The Stank Tower was the next on the section of wall leading to the West Gate. The site of this tower is at the eastern edge of the Central Station portico, near the steps leading down to the Metro Station. We now cross Neville Street to Pink Lane.

The Gunner or Gunnerton Tower near the bottom of Pink Lane is believed to have been built by the Swinburn family, who owned a house behind it. In 1821, it was converted into a hall for the Slaters and Tilers' Company. During the conversion, workmen discovered a large quantity of coins dating to the reign of Edward I, 'Hammer of the Scots'. It is commemorated by the modern Gunner House. A small part of the tower survives but the upper stones of this portion are not the originals.

The Pink Tower stood at the junction of this part of Pink Lane and Clayton Street West. In 1705 the Forth postern was created between this tower and the Gunner Tower for access to

the public recreational space called The Forth. The gate was removed in 1811 and the wall between it and the Gunner Tower demolished. Most of the alleyway (Forth Lane) that led to the postern from Westgate Road survives.

From the Pink Tower the wall ran on to the impressive West Gate, which featured a barbican (fortified outbuilding) and massive oak gates and iron doors. The historian John Leland described the West Gate as 'a mightye strong thinge'. It stood in Westgate Road at its junction with Cross Street and close to the entrance to Bath Lane.

Part of the gate building was used as a prison, sometimes housing unruly apprentices. During the Civil War the gaol contained seventeen prisoners. However, they managed to obtain

Top, the wall between Gunner Tower and Pink Tower. Centre, the remnants of Gunner Tower. Above, Gunner Tower before demolition.

This very early photograph of Pink Tower from the west (possibly during demolition) dates from around 1848.

The West Gate in 1785, by then rather dilapidated.

ropes and, during a stormy night, escaped by letting themselves down via a privy.

Later the West Gate became the meeting hall of the House Carpenters' Company.

In 1811 the West Gate was demolished along with part of the wall on its south side. The 18th century building pictured above became home to the House Carpenters.

According to tradition, this formidably strong entry point to the town was built by Roger Thornton, who was elected mayor of the town on several occasions in the early 1400s. He was also one of the Newcastle representatives in parliaments that met during the reigns of Henry IV and Henry V.

Roger Thornton is said to have been extremely poor when he first came to the town (entering through an earlier West Gate). An old Newcastle saying goes:

At the West Gate came Thornton in
With a hap and a halfpenny and a lambskin.

The enterprising Thornton, who came from Hartburn parish in Northumberland, became very wealthy and was described as 'the richest merchant that ever was dwelling in Newcastle'. Thornton gave endowments to churches of the town and funded the building of the Maison de Dieu (House of God), an almshouse founded in 1412 on the eastern side of the old Town Chamber and Court, later replaced by the Guildhall, on the Quayside.

The almshouse was dedicated to St Catherine. Sometimes referred to as Thornton's Hospital, it housed nine poor men and four poor women. Part of the building was used by the Merchant Adventurers' Company.

Thornton has been described as the 'Dick Whittington' of Newcastle, although Whittington seems to have been from a

31

far more comfortably-off background. Thornton and Whittington were contemporaries, dying within seven years of each other.

Thornton's impressive memorial brass, which depicts Roger and his wife, Agnes, as well as his large family of seven sons and seven daughters, is in Newcastle's St Nicholas Cathedral. The benevolent Newcastle merchant and mayor died in 1429. His name lives on in Thornton Street, just opposite Bath Lane, appropriately near the site of the old West Gate.

The walkway along the top of the wall towards Durham Tower is easy to see in this view towards Thornton Street, 1960.

West Gate to New Gate

Cross Westgate Road to Bath Lane at the southern end of the West Walls, the longest surviving section. The Durham Tower stands out as a well preserved feature along this stretch. It was never used by a craft company but became a military lock-up and later a coal and timber store for an adjoining school. The tower was built in the late 13th century.

The Bath Lane stretch of wall is interrupted by Stowell

Above, Durham Tower. Note the corbels that stick out. They were used to support wooden defensive screens.

Right, the Town Wall alongside Bath Lane from a map of 1788.

Bath Lane was named after the public baths that were built here in 1781. The Cooperative Wholesale Society Building, dating to 1890, was erected on their site.

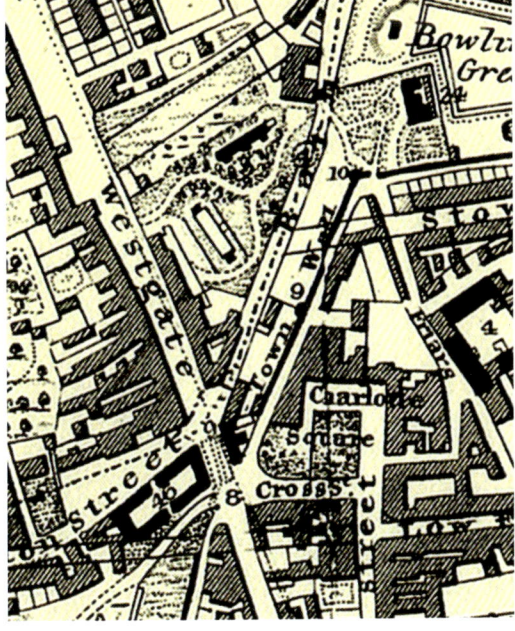

Top, and above, right, both sides of Heber Tower in 1903 when it was in use as a blacksmith's shop, and today, above left, restored. You can see where the door to the shop has been filled in, and the old window has been reinstated.

Street, then turns north at the Heber Tower. The Heber or Herber Tower is generally regarded as the best-preserved tower on the walls. It also dates to the late 13th century.

This building became the meeting place of the Curriers, Armourers and Feltmakers, who repaired it at their own expense in 1620. By the end of the 19th century the building was in use as a blacksmith's shop. Loopholes for firing arrows are still visible.

The rules of the Feltmakers, Curriers and Armourers, dated 1546, included a clause 'that they should not work on holidays, or on Saturdays longer than 5 o'clock in the afternoon, on pain of forfeiting a pound of wax'.

The remains of large stone corbels project from the rounded faces of the Heber and Durham towers. These were used to support wooden screens, which were erected during sieges or

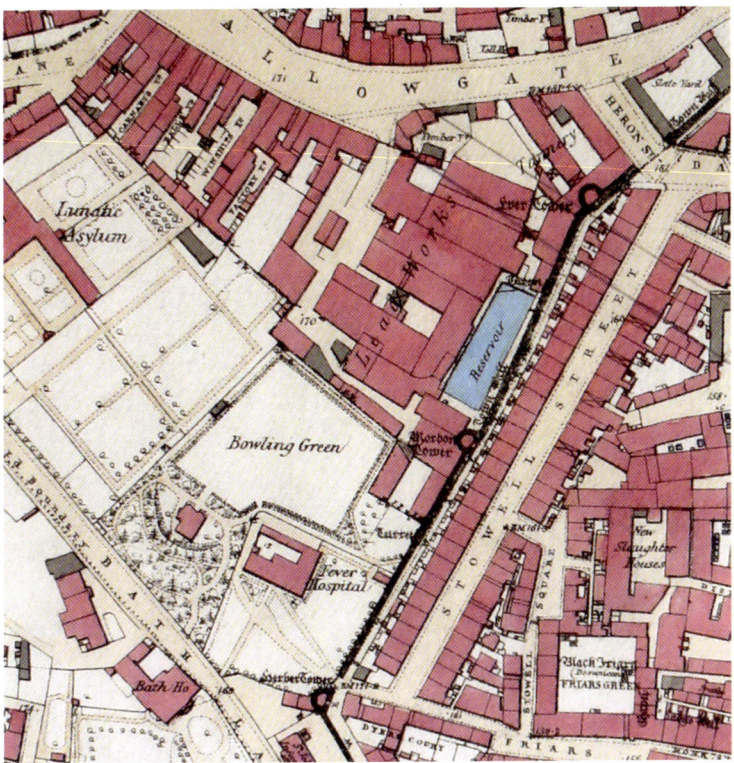

This fascinating section of the First Edition Ordnance Survey map, 1858, shows all the different activities near the Town Walls.

other hostilities. Defenders used their weapons through gaps in the screens.

The fine stretch of the West Walls running onwards behind Stowell Street's China Town towards St Andrew's Street (formerly known as Darn Crook) features two more towers, the Morden and the Ever.

Between the Heber Tower and Morden Tower are two blocked-up doorways. One of these, pictured right, known as the Black Friars' Postern, gave the friars access from their house to their gardens outside the wall. It dates to around 1280 and is marked by a plaque on the town-facing side of the wall in the passage behind Stowell Street. A turret, with the remains of stairs, is also visible on this section. Near this turret is a second postern that dates to the 19th century and gave access to a bowling green beyond the wall.

A prominent feature outside this stretch is the defensive ditch, known as the King's Dyke, but the ditch you see today is not the original one. The Black Friars used a moveable wooden bridge to cross the original dyke. Today's ditch is spanned by a small bridge. The King's Dyke once extended around much of the wall circuit, but infilling and building have erased all traces.

Part of the Black Friars' house, now restored, survives and is well worth a visit. It is a short distance east of Stowell Street and includes the remains of the cloister and foundations of the church. The surviving buildings were once used as a meeting place of the Smiths' Company and eight other craft guilds of the town. The Smiths' motto, today somewhat difficult to read, is inscribed above one of the doorways:

Above, in the second half of the 19th century there was a reservoir associated with the adjoining lead works just beyond the walls. You can see the Morden Tower to the right.

Right, the restored Morden Tower.

Below, beyond the Morden Tower was the entrance to gardens, and the bowling green, seen here in 1886.

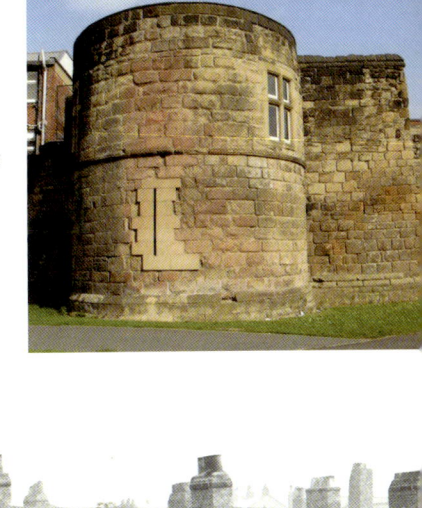

'By hammer and hand
All artes do stand.'

The restored Morden Tower is more or less in the centre of this stretch of the wall. From the early 17th century it was the meeting hall of the Glaziers, Plumbers, Pewterers and Painters. A gilded ball, which was suspended from the centre of the tower ceiling, was believed to have been shot from a Scottish cannon during the siege of 1644. It was probably discovered embedded in the tower wall.

A view of the wall from Morden Tower, back Stowell Street, around 1890.

Rules of the Glaziers, Plumbers and Pewterers, dated 1536, obliged members to 'go together on the Feast of Corpus Christi and maintain their play of *The Three Kings of Coleyn*'. Another rule required that 'no Scotsman born should be taken apprentice, or suffered to work in Newcastle, on pain of forfeiting 3 shillings and 4 pence'. One half of this sum was to go towards the maintenance of the Tyne Bridge.

Since 1964 Morden Tower has become famous for readings by local and international poets.

A fever hospital, opened in 1804 on land once owned by the Black Friars, was a short distance to the west of the wall between the Heber and Morden towers. The hospital was principally for 'the infected poor' but also took some paying patients. The restored three-storey building is close to the re-excavated wall-ditch.

Only the lower part of the Ever Tower can be seen today. It is at the northern end of this stretch of the West Walls, close to the junction of Stowell Street and St Andrew's Street and only yards from the China Town Gate. The tower was built by the family of Ever or Eure, lords of Kirkley, Northumberland, and barons of Witton, County Durham. The Company of Paviours, Colliers and Carriagemen used the Ever Tower during the 19th century. It was partly demolished between 1908 and 1910.

The ruins of another turret – best seen from the passage behind the wall – are visible between the Morden and Ever towers.

The Gallowgate Lead Works once stood immediately outside this section (see the map on page 35). Founded in the late 18th century, it did not close until 1933. The works included a reservoir. The top of a shaft, now capped, can be seen in this area. This deep pit was used for making lead shot.

The line of the wall is now interrupted by St Andrew's Street (Darn Crook) and then continues in the grounds of St Andrew's Church, on the other side of the road. The Andrew Tower once stood here but was demolished when the churchyard was enlarged in 1818. There is a large gap in the wall on the Gallowgate side of the churchyard where the tower once stood.

A old drawing of the wall and tower beside St Andrew's Church.

The remains of a turret can still be seen behind the church, partly embedded in the rear of an adjacent commercial building which fronts on to Gallowgate.

St Andrew's Church is probably the oldest in Newcastle. There is a tradition that it was built by David I of Scotland, to replace an earlier one. David ruled over Newcastle, Northumberland and Cumbria when they were under Scottish control from 1135 to 1157.

During the Civil War siege of 1644 St Andrew's was damaged by Scottish cannon firing from the common land known as Castle Leazes (see the 1639 map on page 21). The church was vulnerable because it was immediately behind the wall. Three cannon balls from this period are on display on a window ledge of the baptistery. They were unearthed in the churchyard.

Unsurprisingly, this area of the wall was breached during the siege, but it was speedily repaired. The defenders are reported to have mounted a gun on top of the church tower and a Scottish preacher was killed by one of its shots while conducting a service.

Running repairs, investigated by Barry Redfern

When Whitefriars Tower was battered by the Scots in 1644 the repairs were recorded in the town accounts books. Recent research has revealed the costs for repairing the tower paid to a Newcastle stone mason:

> **2nd week of April 1645**
> **Paid Tho Tailor mason in full for his worke don at whitefriar Tower wch was battered downe by the Scots vj£ iijs viijd'** *(ie £6 3s 8d)*

In the same month payment of large sums began to the town masons firstly of an agreed sum of £65 to repair damage to the Town Walls:

> **4th week of April 1645**
> **Pd Mr Thomas Tailor maison in pte of 65£ for repareing the Towne Walls as p bill** *(page damaged)*

Between September 1647 and January 1647/1648 (Julian Calendar) it was agreed to pay the masons £95 for further repairs to the Town Walls. The final payment is recorded as:

> **4th weeke of Januarie 1647**
> **pd the masons in full of 95£ ffor repareing ye Towne walls according to agreement as p bill vij£** *(ie £7)*

Later the town authorities began repairs to the town dykes surrounding the wall. The Constables of the wards adjoining the wall were paid to repair the dykes, a typical example being:

> **3rd week of Aprill 1649**
> **Paid Constab of Andrew Tower ward for repareing ye dikes in ye ward xjxs vjd**
> *(ie 19s 6d)*

Many similar entries occur in the account books.

A page from one of Newcastle's account books.

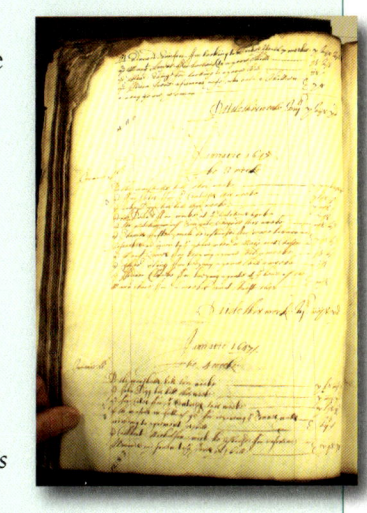

An artist's impression of the Civil War siege.

Below, a very early photograph (around 1848) of St Andrew's churchyard and the Town Wall. It is still recognisable today (right).

R. Bertram

The city's celebrated 18th century composer, Charles Avison (1709-1770) is buried in St Andrew's churchyard, close to the nave porch. Avison, who was organist at St Nicholas Church, composed 50 concertos for stringed orchestra and many sonatas. He was born and died in Newcastle.

Also interred in the churchyard is William Chapman (1749-1832) a civil and mechanical engineer who is now acknowledged as one of the pioneers in the development of the steam locomotive. Chapman also invented the coal drop, a device that improved the loading of ships on the Tyne. Although his gravestone has disappeared, his memorial tablet is in the chancel.

The surviving section of wall at St Andrew's terminates a few yards from Newgate Street. Here, very close to the junction of Newgate Street with Blackett Street and Gallowgate, stood the New Gate. As the name implies, it was probably erected on the site of an earlier gate, which possibly was called the Berwick Gate.

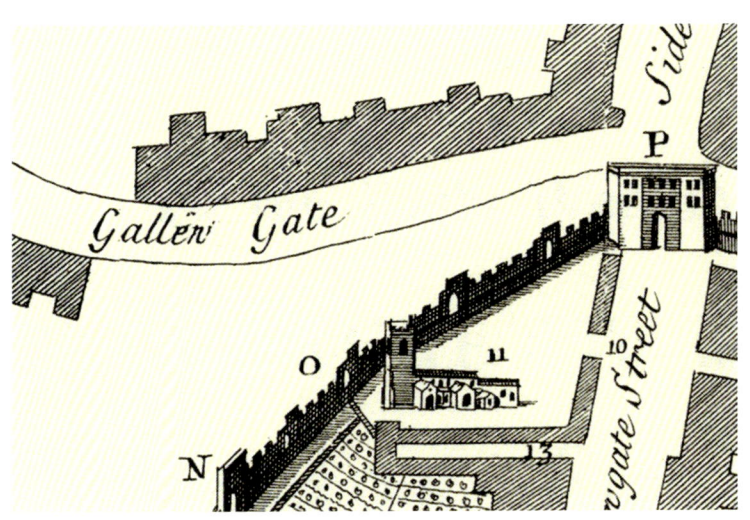

In 1400, Newcastle became a county in its own right, separate from Northumberland. It therefore took custody of its own prisoners and the New Gate became a gaol.

The gate had an outbuilding known as the north front with a gallery on each side through which enemies who had broken in could be attacked. There was also a portcullis.

The New Gate in 1786. It was used as the Town Gaol from around 1400 until 1823. Despite the sturdy gatehouse there were many escapes (including one via a chimney).

Bourne states that it was the strongest and most ancient of the gates. Above the entrance to the north front were three stone shields bearing the Cross of St George and the Arms of England and Newcastle. A statue of a king, possibly James I, stood in an arched niche above the shields.

During the 1644 siege there was fierce fighting close to the gate when Scottish soldiers forced a breach in the walls nearby.

The New Gate was demolished in 1823-24. During the work, several large cannon balls were found embedded deep in the walls.

New Gate to Pilgrim Street Gate

From New Gate the Town Walls ran eastward, approximately along a line a few feet to the south of the southern pavement of Blackett Street, to the Pilgrim Street Gate. This stretch of the defences included two towers, the Bertram Momboucher and the Fickett. Immediately to the north in the area where old Eldon Square and the northern section of Eldon Square shopping centre now stand, lay open fields.

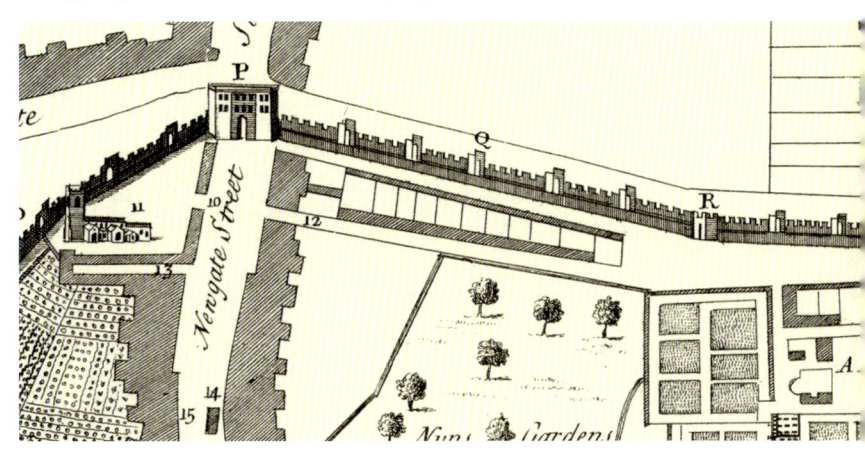

Above, the Town Walls between New Gate and Pilgrim Street Gate in 1736. Q marks the Bertram Momboucher Tower which stood approximately opposite the Eldon Square War Memorial. R marks the Fickett Tower, just about where Grey's Monument is today.

The Bertram Momboucher Tower was named after a High Sheriff of Northumberland during the reigns of Edward III and Richard II. Momboucher owned property in Newcastle.

The Fickett Tower stood near Grey's Monument. In medieval times it was opposite the Grey Friars' Chapel. The house of the Grey Friars, or Franciscans, lay between the northern section of Pilgrim Street and Grey's Monument.

A short distance to the east of the Fickett Tower was the Pilgrim Street Gate at the junction of Pilgrim Street with Blackett Street, New Bridge Street and Northumberland Street. According to popular tradition, pilgrims lodged in the street on their way to and from St Mary's Chapel at Jesmond. They

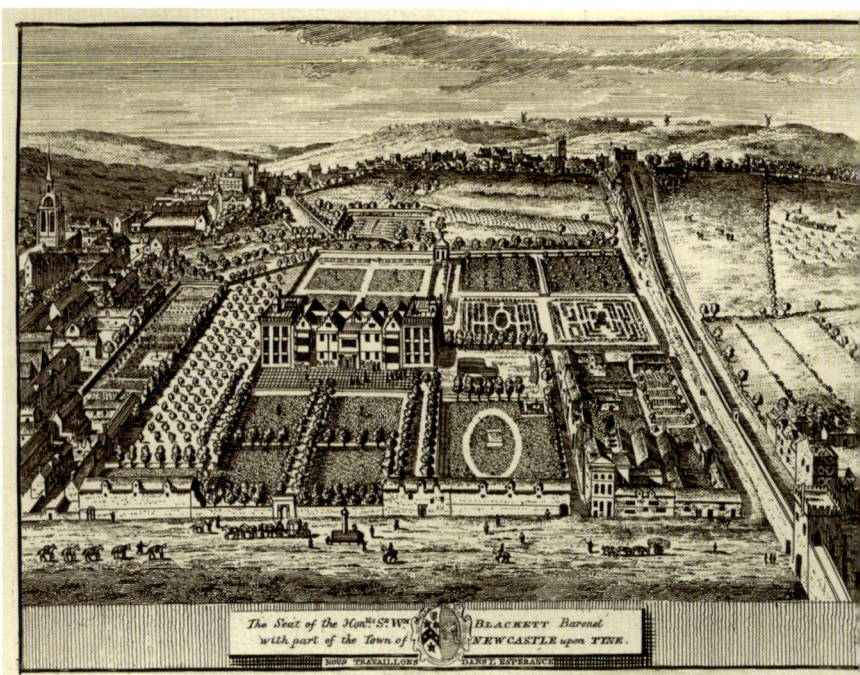

Top, a turret near Fickett Tower from the inside lane beside the walls. Above, the sumptuous Anderson Place before it was removed, along with the Town Walls and towers and the Pilgrim Street Gate, for the redevelopments of the 1820s and 1830s.

Pilgrim Street Gate, 1786.

would have passed through this gate on their journeys.

The Pilgrim Street Gate included a room above the entrance that was used by the Joiners' Company and the entrance was particularly narrow. During demolition of the building in 1802, a large cannon ball was found in the wall about a yard below the battlements. It was almost certainly fired from a Scottish gun during the 1644 siege.

In Grey Street, approximately where the Lloyds TSB Bank building now stands, a large house was built in 1580 by rich merchant Robert Anderson on the land that had belonged to the Franciscans. It was in this mansion, known as the Newe House (and much later as Anderson Place after it was acquired by a different Anderson) that Charles I stayed as a prisoner of the Scots in 1646-47. During this time, he is said to have been allowed to play golf on the Shield Field outside the eastern walls. A plaque on the exterior of the Lloyds TSB Bank building records the connection with Charles I.

Pilgrim Street Gate to Pandon Gate

From Pilgrim Street Gate the wall continued to run eastwards along the line of New Bridge Street to the Carliol Tower, which stood approximately at the junction of today's John Dobson Street and New Bridge Street, immediately next to the City Library.

This tower was named after the Carliols, a family of wealthy Newcastle merchants during the late medieval period. It was refurbished as a meeting place for the Weavers' Company in 1682 and was also known as the Weavers' Tower. There was further improvement work in 1821. Two years later, another large cannon ball from the 1644 siege was found here by workmen creating a window on the north side of the tower. It had lodged some two feet into the wall.

Mackenzie, writing a few years later, states: 'The hall is now extremely commodious, and a turret, containing a staircase, has been annexed to the tower, on which a flag is hoisted on days of rejoicing.'

The tower was demolished in 1880 to clear the site for the building of the new Free Library. Some of the stones from the Carliol Tower are on display in today's City Library which was built approximately on the same spot.

Carliol Tower shortly before its demolition.

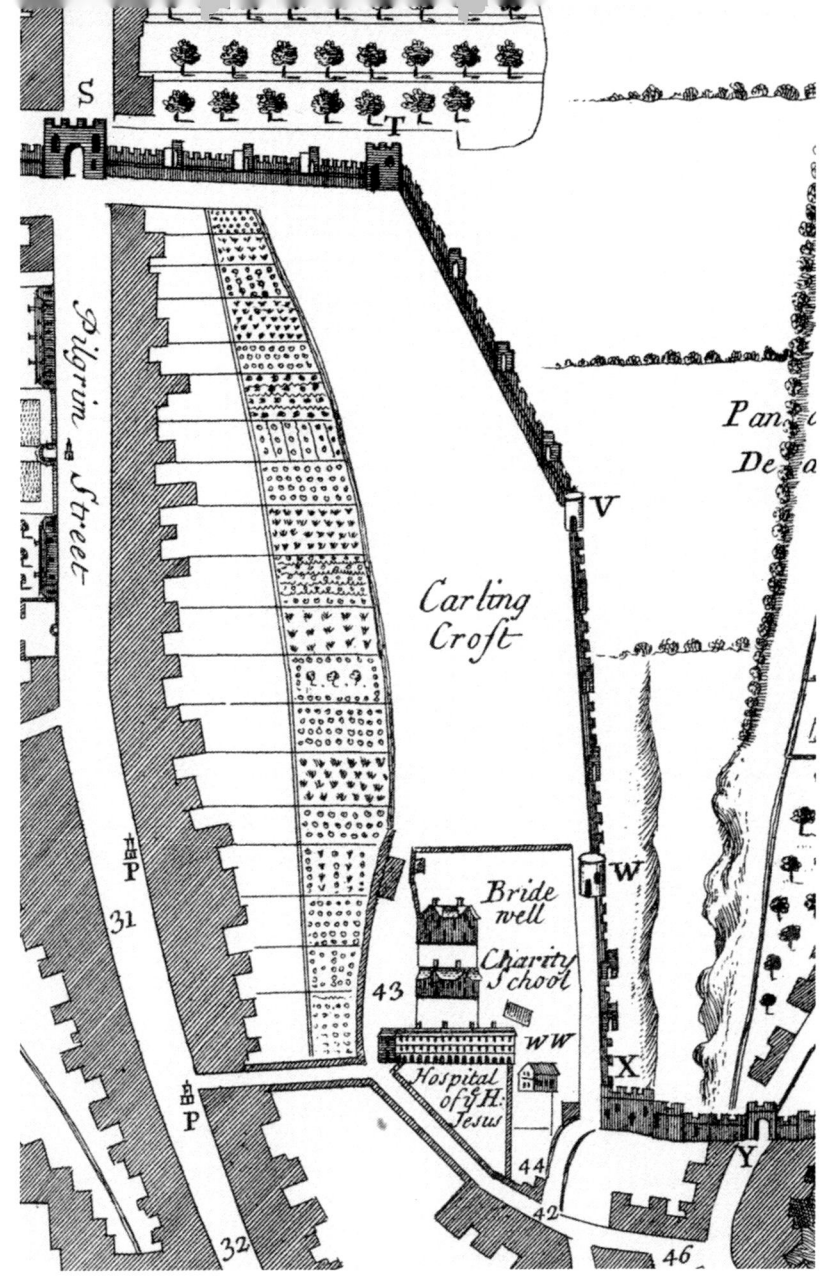

The section of wall between the Pilgrim Street Gate (marked S on this 1736 map) and the Carliol Tower (T) was the site of three small turrets. One was the 'Waits' Tower', a reference to the lively town band that practised there. The musicians wore three-cocked hats and blue cloaks and played at the mayor's official functions, at weddings and at Christmas time. After lasting for centuries, the band seems to have folded during the opening years of the 19th century.

The Weavers' history began long before they occupied the tower. A Weavers' Company document of 1527 required members to 'assemble yearly at the Feast of Corpus Christi, go together in procession, and play their play and pageant of *The Bearing of the Cross*, at their own expense'. Regulations adopted by the Weavers also included a rule 'that any brother falling into poverty should be supplied out of the common box.'

A short distance from the City Library and opposite the Laing Art Gallery is the old Lying-in Hospital. This former maternity unit was opened in 1826 for poor married women and could accommodate only seven patients. It was designed by John Dobson. In 1925 the BBC took the building over, and today it contains offices on Blue Carpet Square.

From the Carliol Tower the wall turned sharply southwards, approximately along a line a few yards east of John Dobson Street, to the Plummer Tower (V on the map on page 49) in Croft Street. Follow the pavement southwards on the eastern side of John Dobson Street and the line would be a little to the left. An open field known as the Carliol, or Carling, Croft ran along the inner part of this section of wall. It was owned by the Carliol family.

If we turn left at the bottom of John Dobson Street and along Market Street East and then take the first right into Croft Street we come to the Plummer Tower, also sometimes referred to as the Carliol Croft Tower or Cutlers' Tower. It dates to the late 13th century. The Plummer family were leading merchants and politicians of the town in the late 13th and 14th centuries.

It was used for meetings by the Cutlers' Company and in 1742 the building was taken over by the Masons' Company who repaired it and gave it a facelift. A new, classical-style façade was built on the town-facing side.

The rules of the Masons' Company, according to a

Opposite, the Plummer Tower, above in 1915, and below, restored.

51

document of 1581, included a clause requiring that 'at the marriages and burials of brethren, or their wives, the company should attend to the church' and that one half of fines exacted from members should go towards the maintenance of the Tyne Bridge, 'and the other half to the said Fellowship'.

Later, the Plummer Tower was used as a private home, then as an annexe of the Laing Art Gallery. Although greatly modified, the D-shape of the tower is still apparent.

A bastion for artillery, installed during the Civil War, was built on to its curved, outward face. A short section of the Town Wall adjoins its south side.

From the Plummer Tower the wall

The rear of Plummer Tower, late 19th century.

If you are following the walk around the walls and towers, at this point retrace your steps to Blue Carpet Square and the Laing Art Gallery. Turn right and climb the wooden spiral stairs to reach the footbridge over the motorway. Once you have crossed, turn right down the stairs and at the bottom bear left across the road to Trafalgar Street and carry on down the hill beneath the railway viaduct. This mighty arch was built in 1847-8 for the Newcastle and Berwick Railway. Cross Melbourne Street, then City Road, to arrive at the Corner Turret. (See map on inside front cover.)

continued to run southward, crossing the site of the Central Motorway to the Austin Tower, which was close to where the Manors multi-storey car park is today. This tower was so called because it was near the Austin Friary. The friars' buildings were immediately behind the car park.

Following the Dissolution of the Monasteries in the 16th century, Henry VIII kept the buildings of the Austin Friary for the use of the King's Council of the North, if needed. This area became known as Manors, taking its name from the King's Manor.

Holy Jesus Hospital stands directly on the site of the Austin Friars' Church. The hospital was founded in 1681 to provide for poor freemen

Austin Tower around 1890.

Holy Jesus Hospital, which is accessible from City Road, or the pedestrian subway from Pilgrim Street.

of the town or their widows and unmarried children. Behind it is a 16th century tower. A small section of the church wall, with a medieval window, is visible inside the hospital, between it and the tower.

The now vanished Austin Tower was used as the meeting hall of the Millers and Coopers and afterwards the Ropers. In Mackenzie's time the lower apartment was converted into stables.

From the Austin Tower the wall ran south eastwards to the Corner Turret, sometimes called Corner Tower, in City Road. Here there was a commanding view down the lower part of Pandon Dene towards the river. It is still a good vantage point, overlooking Broad Chare and the Tyne.

At both sides of this turret, which is actually two turrets at right angles to one another, are two short sections of wall. The more easterly section, much overgrown, is very close to the multi-storey car park on City Road.

At the Corner Turret the builders of the Town Wall were forced to rethink their plans. Instead of continuing directly south towards the river, it was decided to turn the wall 90 degrees east, to incorporate the village of Pandon, which had been absorbed into the town in 1298-99.

This 1882 view is from near the Pandon Gate. Corner Turret is on the hill.

Above, Corner Turret in 1966.

Right, a section of the wall can be seen below the Corner Turret behind Pandon carpark.

55

The wall dropped down the steep slope to the Pandon Gate, which stood near the possible line of the Roman Wall in this part of the city. An old Newcastle saying was: 'As old as Pandon Gate' and some historians believed that the structure contained Roman elements, perhaps incorporating a Roman turret, or that such a turret stood nearby. It is possible that stones from Hadrian's Wall were used in building the gate. The entrance itself had iron doors. The site of Pandon Gate is in front of the City Road multi-storey car park, below Pandon Bank.

The gate was an early meeting place of the town's Barber Surgeons. In 1648, following damage to one of its walls during the Civil War, they petitioned Newcastle Corporation for a new meeting hall and land for a garden in which to grow medicinal herbs. They were granted a site for a new hall at the former Austin Friary at Manors and a portion of the friars' garden to plant their herbs. Today, the garden and hall have vanished under the railway viaduct, but the Barber Surgeons' Gardener's Cottage still stands next to the Corner Turret.

The Pandon Gate.

Above, the Barber Surgeons' Hall, and garden, Manors.

Right, the Gardener's Cottage in the early 20th century.

Below, The Gardener's Cottage today.

This drawing from around 1590 is one of the earliest representations of Newcastle, and the drop of the Town Wall at Pandon can be clearly seen. (British Library: Cott.Aug.i.vol.ii.4)

(Reproduced from Mackenzie's History of Newcastle.)

Pandon Gate to Sand Gate

From Pandon Gate, the Town Walls ran approximately eastwards uphill to Sallyport Tower (also known as the Wall Knoll Tower because it stands on a hill, or knoll) which included the Sallyport Gate, a postern from which sorties ('sallies') could be made by defenders during sieges.

The Sallyport Tower is also sometimes referred to as the Carpenters' Tower because the Shipwright Carpenters held their meetings here. During the early 18th century these craftsmen had the upper part of the tower (which had been badly damaged during the Civil War siege of 1644) removed and constructed a square tower on top of the lower section. Four small turrets were fitted to its roof. It is this greatly modified tower that can be seen today.

The Shipwrights embellished one side of the building with a stone carving of a ship's hull which can still be seen

Top, Sallyport Tower. It is accessible from Garth Heads, just off City Road, or from Tower Street. Above, a view of the tower from Pandon in 1880.

today. They repaired and maintained vessels that called into the Tyne to collect coal and other cargoes, but they also built ships.

The former All Hallows' Church, which was demolished in the late 18th century to make way for All Saints' Church above the Quayside, contained the tomb of Thomas Wrangham, who seems to have been a very successful 17th century shipbuilder.

His inscription tablet recorded: 'Under the adjacent marble is interred the body of Thomas Wrangham, the famous and beloved shipbuilder of this town … He built five and forty sail of ships and died of fever in the 42nd year of his age, May 26th 1689.'

The tower stands close to the Keelmen's Hospital in City Road. Newcastle's keelmen conveyed coal from the North East mines down the Tyne to the sailing ships waiting in Shields Harbour. Keels – small flat-bottomed boats – were a familiar sight on the river for hundreds of years. As long as ships had difficulties sailing up the Tyne to collect coal, these little vessels were essential. They became obsolete during the second half of the 19th century after the River Tyne was improved by dredging.

The keelmen formed a charity in 1697-99 to build the hospital which opened in 1701 as a residential home for elderly, sick or infirm keelmen and their widows. The working keelmen paid for it themselves at the cost of £2,000 (fourpence per journey was deducted from their wages). Dr John Moore, Bishop of Ely, said of the Keelmen's Hospital that 'he had heard of and seen many hospitals, the works of rich men; but that it was the first he had ever seen or heard of that had been built by the poor'. It is a Grade II listed building.

From the Sallyport Tower the wall veered downhill south-eastwards and then south to the Sand Gate, close to the riverside. This almost certainly was named after the sandy shore of this stretch of the river. It was taken down in 1798.

It was in the district immediately outside the Sand Gate, centred on the street known as Sandgate, that most of the town's keelmen lived. They and the gate were immortalised in

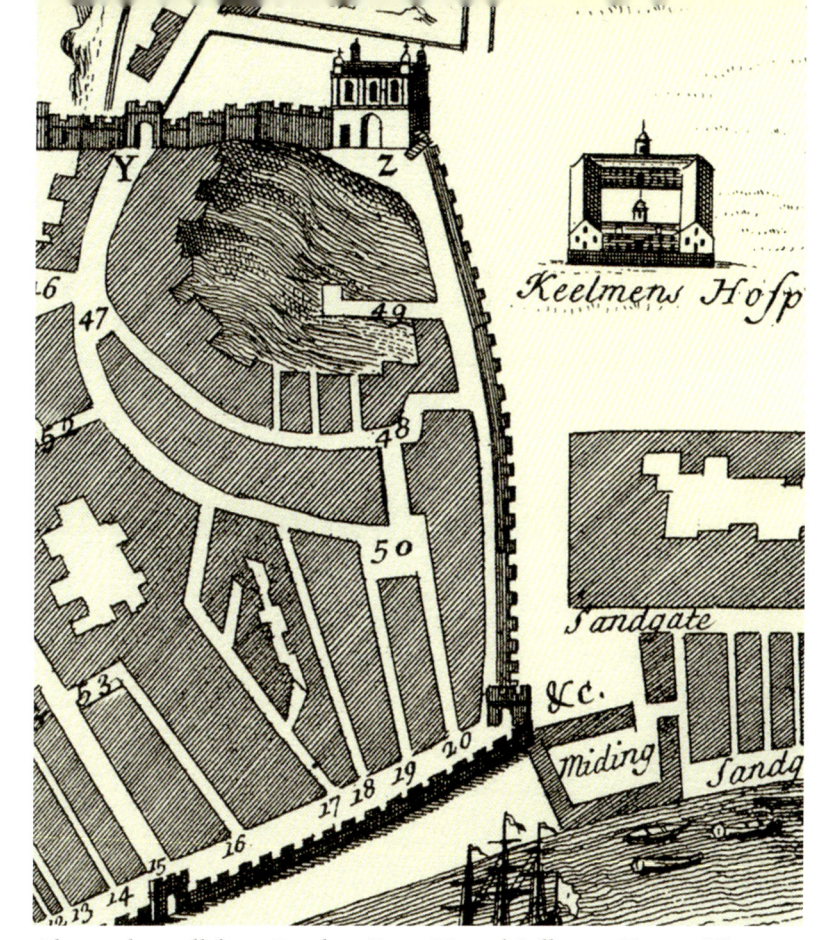

Above, the wall from Pandon Gate (Y) and Sallyport Tower (Z) to Sand Gate in 1736. Below, the Keelmen's Hospital.

61

the Newcastle song, *The Keel Row*:

*As I came through Sand Gate, through Sand Gate,
Through Sand Gate,
As I came through Sand Gate
I heard a lassie sing:
'Weel may the keel row,
the keel row, the keel row.
Weel may the keel row,
that ma laddie's in'.*

*Above, Sand Gate in the 18th century.
Below, the street known as Sandgate around 1890.*

Sand Gate to Close Gate

Leaving the Sand Gate, the wall turned back sharply westwards along the Quayside. It was here that many water gates gave people access through the wall to the ships moored at the quay. From the reign of James I onwards most were locked at night. However, two were kept open to enable captains and seamen to pass to and from their vessels.

Top, the Quayside, 1745. Above, a similar perspective today. Note the Sallyport Tower and the Keelmen's Hospital on both views.

A careful watch was kept on these night gates. Bourne says that this was done to prevent servants and others from casting ashes into the river, although the security of the town was another good reason for such vigilance.

This section of wall ended at the eastern end of Roger Thornton's Maison de Dieu. An 18th century illustration (below) shows the line of the wall turning at a slight angle and rising to merge with the Maison's main structure.

This drawing of the Quayside Town Wall is dated to 10 January 1763, shortly before demolition.

By the 18th century the riverside wall was regarded as a hindrance to business on the river and the passage of carriages. It was demolished in 1763 and some of its stones were used to build the elegant St Ann's Church on City Road.

A modern wall, featuring a relief of the River Tyne and some of its bridges and landmarks, follows part of the line of the old Quayside section, running westwards from where the Sand Gate stood.

The Bridge End Gate was at the north end of the Tyne Bridge, completed in around 1250. This bridge may have replaced an 11th or 12th century bridge said to have been destroyed by fire in around 1248. There is no clear evidence that this earlier crossing existed, but if it did, it may have been constructed at about the time that the New Castle was rebuilt

The old Tyne Bridge, shortly after the flood of 1771.

in stone in the 1100s.

The Tyne Bridge of around 1250 was lined with shops and houses at the Gateshead end and there was a chapel dedicated to St Thomas the Martyr (Thomas Becket) at its Newcastle end. Two gateway towers were built on the bridge, one of these close to the Gateshead end and the other between the third and fourth arches from the Newcastle side. The Newcastle tower was used for a number of years as a prison. Other features of the bridge included a chapel and a hermitage that housed a priest who was left six marks a year by Roger Thornton to pray for the latter's soul.

The bridge lasted for over 500 years, but in 1339 it was badly damaged by a flood and 120 people were drowned. Despite this disaster, it survived and was repaired.

In 1636, a gateway tower, known as the Magazine Gate (right), was built at the northern end of the bridge. This was probably because the old Bridge End Gate had fallen into decay and been removed. The town's gunpowder, and perhaps weapons, were kept there.

A rare photograph of the 1781 Tyne Bridge before 1866. A notice warns there is 'NO PASSAGE UNDER BRIDGE'.

In 1771, a major flood swept large sections of the old Tyne Bridge away, including many of the shops and houses. Five people were drowned and two were reported to have died afterwards of 'fright'. The structure was beyond repair.

Its replacement, a stone bridge with nine low arches, was opened in 1781. Despite its sturdy construction and elegant looks, by the mid 19th century it had become an impediment to industrial development because most ships were unable to pass under the low arches. It was demolished and the Swing Bridge built in the same position.

The new structure was 'shipping-friendly'. The Swing Bridge, with its ability to open and close, enabled large vessels to pass up and down the Tyne to and from reaches above Newcastle Quayside. It was completed in 1876, opening the way for colliers (coal-carrying cargo steamers) and large warships built at Armstrong's works at Elswick.

The Guildhall and Exchange, which is very close to the sites of the Bridge End Gate and St Thomas's Chapel, was built between 1655 and 1658. Designed by Robert Trollope, it was the centre of the town's administration and justice.

Alterations were made in the late 18th and early 19th centuries to form the Guildhall that you see today. The last of these alterations, by John Dobson, included the demolition of the adjoining Maison de Dieu and its replacement with a new,

Top, Robert Trollope's Guildhall. Above, the Guildhall in 1928.

The panelled Mayor's Parlour of the Guildhall.

semi-circular east end. This featured a fish market with a colonnaded front on the ground floor. Above the fish market a replacement Merchant Adventurers' Court was built, which is still there today and contains some of the finely carved 17th century oak woodwork rescued from the old merchants' court.

Further modifications to the building were completed in the late 19th century. However, the 17th century Mayor's Parlour and Town Court survive behind the extensively remodelled exterior. It was in the Mayor's Parlour that the Common Council met and key decisions concerning the town were made. The Town Court (also known as the Guildhall) was an important venue for meetings as well as a courtroom where trials took place.

The 17th century Guildhall and Exchange superseded a medieval centre of administration and justice on the same site comprising the Town Chamber (sometimes referred to as the Town House) in which the government of the town's affairs and management of revenues were conducted, and the first Town Court. Below the Court was the Exchange and weigh-house where trade took place.

In his classic work, *Newcastle Town* (1885) historian R.J.

Charlton tells us that when the Maison de Dieu (see the picture on page 64) was demolished in 1823 the remains of a stretch of the Town Wall foundations were discovered underneath.

A bustling Sandhill scene at the beginning of the last century. The Guildhall is on the left.

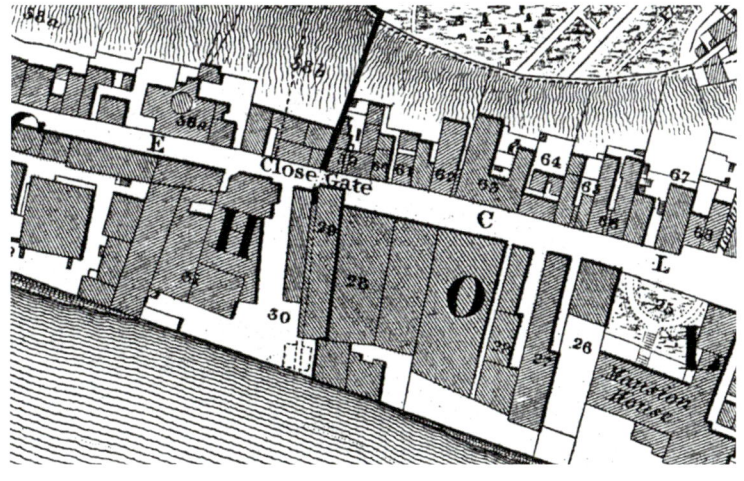

From the nearby Bridge End Gate the wall should, in theory, have run west along the river bank to the Riverside Tower but recent excavations contradict this idea. The wall ran east from the Riverside Tower for a short distance and ended approximately in line with the site of the 17th century Mansion House, above, lower right.

Perhaps it was not considered vital to complete the defensive line here, as the bridge, the slopes of the Tyne Gorge and buildings close to the riverside provided an adequate barrier without blocking access to the river.

Newcastle's famously strong walls did not completely surround the town.

A Mystery Wall?

Intriguingly, it is possible that Newcastle had an earlier Town Wall, predating the one begun in the late 13th century.

The medieval antiquarian and chronicler John Harding (1378-1465) seems to have believed that it was built during the reign of William Rufus (William II), a son of William the Conqueror. A charter of 1216, near the end of John's reign, refers to the existence of a wall.

However, some believe that the charter may be referring to repairs or renewal of the New Castle curtain wall rather than to a wall around the town. It should be noted that Harding was writing around 300 years after the time of William Rufus.

Mackenzie says that it was 'certain' the town was walled in the reign of King John and that the 1216 charter 'expressly mentioned' the wall. Modern historians and archaeologists think it extremely unlikely that it existed.

Remains of the castle's curtain wall south of the Castle Keep. A well-preserved stretch of this wall can be accessed from Castle Stairs and from the rear of the Bridge Hotel.

Newcastle's Civil War Siege

In 1644, during the Civil War, a Scottish Covenanter army of around 30,000, commanded by Alexander Leslie, Earl of Leven, besieged and bombarded Newcastle. The royalist mayor, Sir John Marley, led the 1,700 defenders. They held out for ten weeks against these great odds.

The approach of the Scots had been expected and William Cavendish, Marquis of Newcastle, at this time governor of the town, drafted in extra soldiers to strengthen the garrison. He ordered some of the suburbs outside the northern and south eastern walls to be set on fire to prevent the enemy using them as cover. Sandgate was one of the districts chosen.

The Scottish general moved onwards with the majority of his army, leaving several regiments to keep an eye on the town. He captured Sunderland and South Shields and later took his forces south to take part in the Battle of Marston Moor, near York.

Deadly enemies. Above, Sir William Cavendish, royalist Marquis of Newcastle. Top, Alexander Leslie, Earl of Leven.

A view from the Windmill Hills around 1868. It commands a good position above Newcastle. The Scots placed cannon here.

Marston Moor was resounding victory for Parliament, to which the Scottish army was allied. In August, Leven returned north to begin the main siege of Newcastle.

By this time, the Earl of Callander had arrived on the banks of the Tyne, having crossed the border with 10,000 men to reinforce Leven's army.

Callander made his headquarters at Gateshead after dislodging royalist forces from the Windmill Hills area. According to Mackenzie he 'chased them down the Gatesyde, and hushing them along the bridge, closed them within the town'.

Several of Callander's regiments crossed the Tyne a little below the Ouseburn using a bridge of keels and set up positions outside the eastern walls. Callander placed five batteries of cannon on the Gateshead side.

Leven also crossed the Tyne using a bridge of keels and set up his headquarters at Elswick on the western side of the walls. He spread his forces along the western and northern outskirts. The town was now surrounded and subjected to regular cannon bombardment.

Cannon fire did not force the defenders into submission. On several occasions Leven called upon the mayor, aldermen and

Cannon balls from the Civil War on show in the Castle Keep.

burgesses to surrender to avoid further bloodshed, but this was always refused.

Many people were killed, although we don't know the exact number, and there was extensive damage to buildings including All Saints and St Andrew's churches. Unsurprisingly, there were a considerable number of people in the town who thought surrender would have been the wisest course.

The Scots were almost certainly aware of the discontent amongst some sections of the population and shot leaflets over the walls in an attempt to persuade townspeople that they should press the mayor to surrender.

William Lithgow, a well-travelled Scot who was present at the siege, was impressed by the Town Walls. He wrote: 'The walls here of Newcastle are a great deal stronger than those of York, and not unlike to the walls of Avignon, but especially of Jerusalem; being all three decorated about the battlements with little quadrangled turrets; the advantage resting only with Newcastle in regard of seventeen dungeon towers fixt about the walls (and they also wonderfully strong), which the other two have not …'

In his account of the siege, Lithgow describes in detail the way the walls were heavily fortified by the defenders. For

An artist's impression of the siege.

instance, he states that 'all the gapes of the battlements were shut up with lime and stone, having a narrow slit in them through which they might murder our soldiers and secure themselves from a just revenge'. We learn that the exterior base of the walls was 'steeply lined with clay mixed with earth to intercept any footing for ladders or climbing thereon'.

Other defensive measures included the construction of an earthwork fort outside the walls at Shieldfield, 'standing on a moderate height and champion-like, commanding the fields'. This fort had been built a short time before the enemy's arrival in February and had defied a Scottish attempt to capture it. In addition, the Castle was strengthened and cannon placed on top of the Keep.

A view from Shieldfield around 1780 shows the walls from Carliol Tower to the Corner Turret. A strong defence.

Lithgow describes Newcastle's defenders: '... they were but 800 of the trained band and some 900 besides of volunteers, pressed men, colliers, keelmen and poor tradesmen, with some few experimental officers to overtop them, which were at last overtopped themselves'.

The Scottish forces threatened to demolish the tower of St Nicholas Church by directing their cannon fire towards it. However, Sir John Marley shrewdly placed Scottish prisoners in the tower and the threat was never carried out.

Mackenzie tells us that the garrison used 'every effort' to annoy the besiegers. He states: 'In frequent sallies from the postern gates they stormed the trenches of the Scots, who were kept perpetually on the alert in order to repel these desperate attacks.'

Lord Sinclair's regiment, which was stationed between the Shield Field Fort and the Sallyport Tower, 'was distinguished for their activity and courage in repelling the furious sallies of the garrison'.

A tremendous struggle took place for control of the bridge. Mackenzie says the Scots eventually succeeded in establishing themselves along a little over half of it, but the town garrison defended it 'with great gallantry'. The Scots were unable to penetrate any further along the bridge as they were subjected to a bombardment from the cannon on the Half Moon Battery, an artillery position on a semi-circular bastion of the Castle Yard, next to the old Moot Hall.

Leven was exasperated by the constant refusal to surrender. Representatives of the two sides met in an attempt to reach an

Sir John Marley's statue on Northumberland Street.

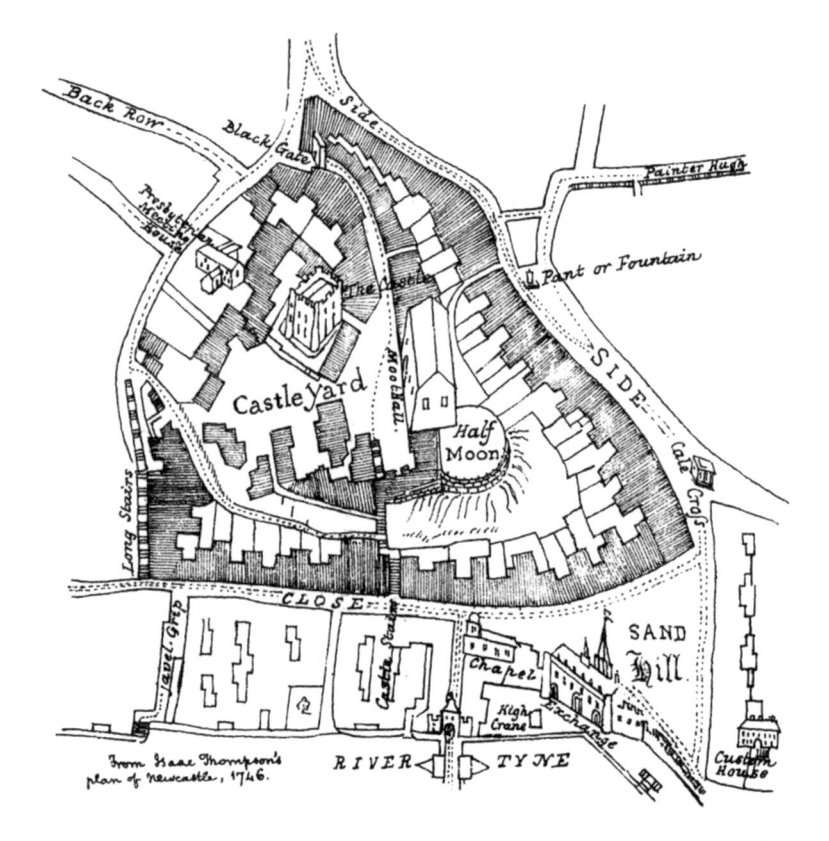

agreement, but the talks ended in deadlock. The Scots blamed Marley's obstinacy.

The turning point came when the defiant mayor sent a letter to Leven which seemed to imply that the Scottish commander was dead, although it is unlikely the mayor ever seriously believed this to be the case. Leven's death was strongly rumoured within the town. The letter proved to be a catalyst.

Marley wrote: 'My Lord, I have received diverse letters and warrants subscribed by the name of Leven, but of late can hear of none that have seen such a man; besides, there is a strong report that he is dead: therefore to remove all scruples, I desire our drummer may deliver one letter to himself. Thus, wishing you could think of some other course to compose the differences of these sad distracted kingdoms than by battering Newcastle, and annoying us who never wronged any of you, for if you seriously consider, you will find that these courses will aggravate and not moderate distempers.'

Leven was far from amused by this message. The next day,

October 19, 1644, the Scottish launched their final assault. They used prolonged cannon bombardment and mines planted with gunpowder, which were driven under the walls by Elswick and Benwell pitmen. Several breaches were made in the walls. For around two hours the townsmen and royalist soldiers defended these gaps against overwhelming odds.

The breaches were near several of the important gates and towers – the Whitefriar Tower, West Gate, Close Gate, New Gate, the Carliol Tower and Sand Gate.

The Scots eventually gained the upper hand, forcing their way into the town. Mackenzie says that at the breach near the Whitefriar Tower defenders on horseback charged the attackers three times, but when reserves arrived the Scots poured into the streets.

On the south eastern side of the walls, Callander and his soldiers climbed through a breach near the Sand Gate and advanced to the Sandhill with 'colours flying and roaring drums'.

According to Mackenzie 'numerous fugitives' from the walls had retreated to the Sandhill, and now, finding themselves surrounded by the enemy, 'laid down their arms and called for quarters' (asked for mercy).

Men holding out at the Pilgrim Street Gate put up a strong resistance, being among the last to surrender. Other major flashpoints of the desperate hand-to-hand fighting were at the breach near the Carliol Tower, where many officers and soldiers of the garrison were killed, and close to the New Gate where a garrison captain fought with his men 'until surrounded by an overwhelming force'.

Even after the Scots had captured the town, Sir John Marley and around 300 defenders – including a group of royalist Scottish nobles and gentry – held out in the Castle Keep for a few days longer before surrendering.

There was rejoicing in London at news of the town's capitulation. Parliament had considered it vital that Newcastle be taken to ensure resumption of coal supplies to the capital.

After the siege, some of the townspeople blamed Marley for

the loss of life and destruction, that, they pointed out, had resulted from his refusal to surrender earlier. Mackenzie tells us that immediately after surrendering the 'gallant mayor was almost torn to pieces by the mob'.

Sir John was imprisoned in the castle for a while and then sent to the Tower of London. He managed to escape to the Continent.

To the credit of Leven, and his army, it seems there was no slaughter of townspeople and no major pillaging after the surrender, although there was some plundering of poorer homes. Mackenzie says that the town's hutch (large strong box) was rifled and a number of documents destroyed. William Lithgow was 'ravished with admiration to behold how in the heat of blood and goring slaughter they got so soon mercie and quarters'. Afterwards, Parliament provided money for repair of the damaged walls.

Historic ammunition: top, a pottery hand grenade; above, musket balls, on show in the Castle Keep.

Following the restoration of the monarchy in 1660, Newcastle began using the motto 'Fortiter Defendit Triumphans' – 'Triumphing by a Brave Defence', believed to have been conferred upon the town by Charles I. Although

Newcastle had been captured by the Scots, it seems that Charles felt the royalist townspeople and soldiers had triumphed in spirit. Sir John Marley lived to tell the tale – he was reinstated as mayor.

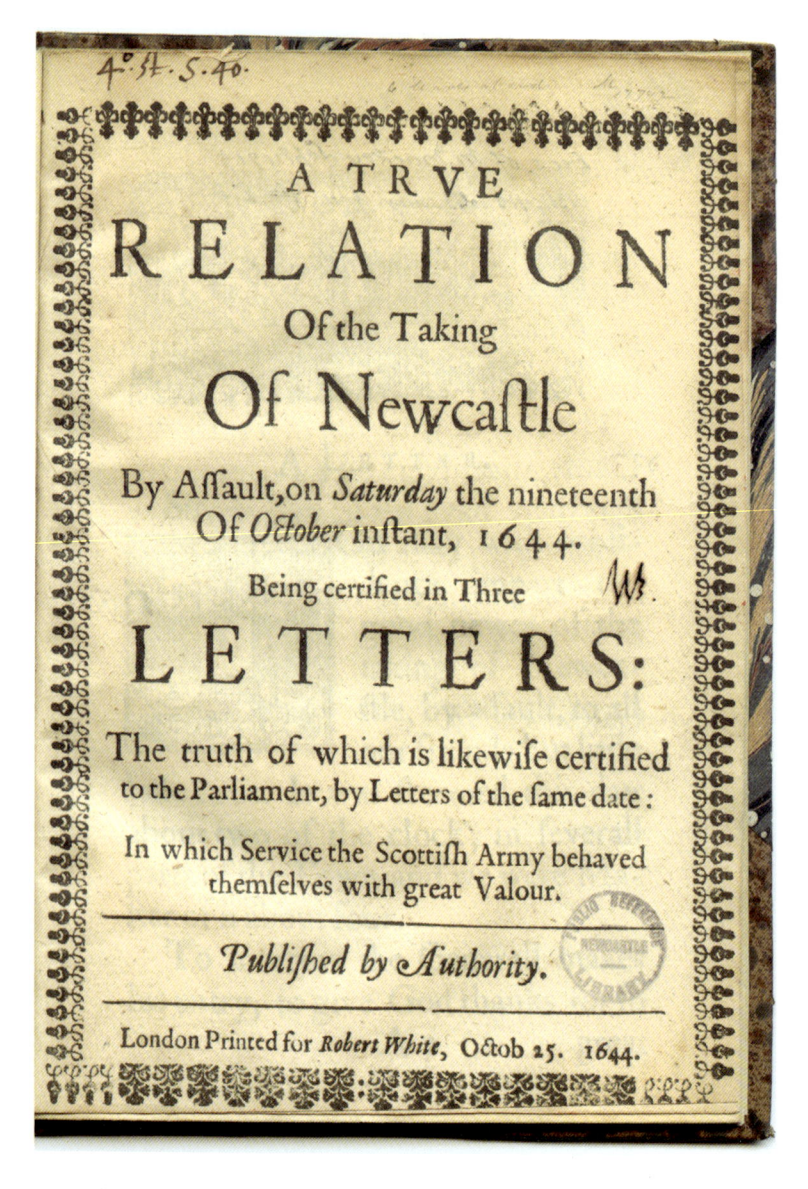

A TRUE RELATION Of the Taking Of Newcastle By Assault, on *Saturday* the nineteenth Of *October* instant, 1644.

Being certified in Three LETTERS:

The truth of which is likewise certified to the Parliament, by Letters of the same date:

In which Service the Scottish Army behaved themselves with great Valour.

Published by Authority.

London Printed for *Robert White*, Octob 25. 1644.

From the collection of Civil War tracts at Newcastle City Library. These documents bring to life the drama and the violent struggle that took place here in 1644.

Geordies and Jacobites

By the 18th century the Town Walls were decaying. Despite this, cannon were placed on them again in 1745 when it was feared that Bonnie Prince Charlie (Charles Edward Stuart) and his Highlanders would threaten the town. They never came, but captured Carlisle instead.

In the first Jacobite rebellion of 1715 the Newcastle townspeople were strong supporters of George I and the House of Hanover. Most of the leading citizens were firmly opposed to any return of the Stuart dynasty. Hundreds of keelmen had volunteered to defend the town and be ready at half an hour's notice should there be an attack on the walls. The gates were sealed with stone.

The defeat of the Jacobites in 1715 was followed by thirty years without a major effort to restore the Stuarts. Then came the shock of the 1745 rebellion during the reign of George II.

The Jacobite victory at Prestonpans, near Edinburgh, in which General Sir John Cope's troops were routed by the Highlanders, caused many to think that an attack on Newcastle was imminent. It was expected that Bonny Prince Charlie would attempt to capture the town as he swept southwards on the East Coast route. Even before Cope's defeat, 800 leading citizens had declared their

These figures once stood on a turret of the Town Walls as a warning. They are preserved in the Garrison Room of the Castle Keep.

allegiance to George II. The town's militia had mounted guard on the walls. Wealthy residents fled to the countryside, taking their most valuable possessions with them.

Preparations were made to repulse an assault. Around 200 cannon were placed on the Town Walls. The main gates were walled up. Several of the water gates were also sealed, but provided with gun holes. At night, fires were lit in the area immediately outside the walls to enable enemies to be seen should they approach too closely to the town. As in 1715, there was no shortage of volunteers to serve as defenders.

Meanwhile, Hanoverian soldiers began arriving in Newcastle. Eventually an army of 15,000, commanded by Field-Marshal George Wade, was encamped on the Town Moor.

It was reported that around 1,000 of Bonny Prince Charlie's Highlanders had approached within seventeen miles of Newcastle. However, the Jacobite force had been dispatched as a ruse in an attempt to confuse Wade. Bonny Prince Charlie had decided to capture Carlisle, not Newcastle. Mackenzie stated that the 'formidable' preparations of the town against an assault had caused the enemy to avoid Newcastle.

After taking Carlisle, the main body of Highlanders set off south, with London as their target. They never reached the capital. Instead, they turned around at Derby and retreated north. Unsurprisingly, there was rejoicing in Newcastle when the Jacobite army was finally defeated at Culloden, near Inverness, in 1746.

According to one popular belief, the people of Tyneside are known as Geordies because of the strong allegiance of Newcastle to George I and George II during the two rebellions. However, that allegiance was never put to the final test and the Town Walls never saw a shot fired in anger during these times.

This detail from an engraving of Anderson Place in the 18th century shows the formidable barrier the Town Wall presented to the North. The Pilgrim Street Gate is bottom right.

The New Castle

Newcastle is so named after the New Castle built in 1080 on the orders of Robert Curthose, eldest son of William the Conqueror, following his return from a military foray into Scotland. This stronghold would probably have been a typical, early Norman castle featuring ditches and surrounded by a wooden palisade. There might also have been an earth mound (motte) with a wooden Keep at its top.

Robert Curthose chose an excellent position for his castle. To the south lay the precipitous slopes that fall away to the River Tyne and to the north and east there is the steep valley (or dene) of the Lort Burn, a tributary of the Tyne. To the west there is flatter land, but a ditch provided extra protection on this side.

The Romans also appreciated the defensive value of the location, for it was here that they built their fort to guard the bridge. The Normans erected their stronghold on the site of the Roman one.

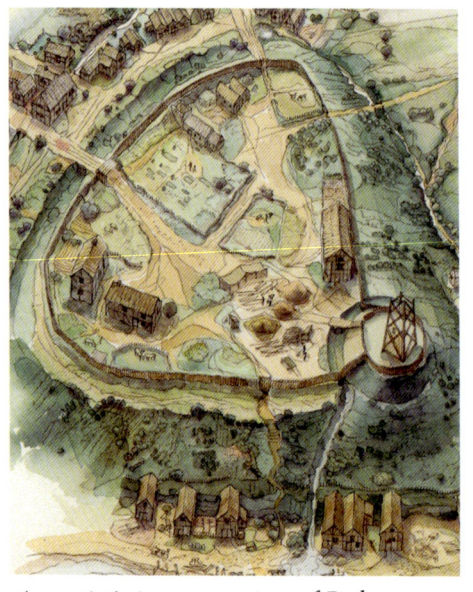

An artist's interpretation of Robert Curthose's wooden new castle.

The remains of the Roman fort of Pons Aelius lie under and adjacent to the Castle Keep.

During the Anglo-Saxon period – when the settlement was possibly known as Monkchester – the fort site was used as a cemetery. The earliest burials date to around 700 AD. Traces of

The remains of the Roman fort of Pons Aelius lie under and beside the Castle Keep. Part of the headquarters building, the commanding officer's house and a granary were found next to the Keep and a second granary under one of the railway arches. Their outlines have been marked out on cobbled pavement areas that cover the remains.

what might have been a Saxon church have been found near the railway arches between the Keep and the Black Gate.

Only fifteen years after the New Castle was built it saw military action. In 1095, Robert de Mowbray, Earl of Northumbria, rebelled against William Rufus and took over the fortress. The king came northwards with his forces to crush the revolt and recaptured the castle after a siege.

Robert Curthose's earth and timber castle was replaced with a stone one during the reign of Henry II. This much stronger fortress was built between 1168 and 1178. Its architect was a man known to history as 'Maurice the Engineer.' Henry II must have been pleased with his work, for Maurice would later be responsible for the construction of Dover Castle.

The second 'New Castle' was built of sandstone and featured a strong, approximately square-shaped Keep. The Castle Keep – constructed between 1172 and 1177 – is one of the city's oldest major buildings. Its walls are up to 18ft thick.

The Keep is entered via steep stairs that lead to a forebuilding with small towers. Arranged on three floors, the interior of the Keep includes a great hall, private apartments known as the King's Chamber and Queen's Chamber (names given them in the 19th century) and a chapel. The well in the Keep, essential during sieges, is nearly 100ft deep.

The ground floor, today known as the Garrison Room, was used as a prison and contains a number of important historical artefacts. These

Anthony Flowers

Geoff Laws

Above, *a reconstruction of the Keep at the end of the 12th century.*

86

Two views of the Castle Keep and the surrounding area before the embellishments of the early 19th century changed its look by adding the four corner towers we know today, with their crenellations.

*Top, the Bluestone boundary from the old Tyne Bridge.
Above left, the crest of the Bishop of Durham, and right, the seahorses of Newcastle's crest.*

include two statues of armed warriors or knights, now headless, which stood on a turret of the Town Walls; a stone panel from the New Gate, bearing the Royal Arms of England on a shield; two stone panels featuring the coats of arms of the Bishop of Durham and of Newcastle from the towers on the medieval Tyne Bridge; and the Bluestone, which stood on the bridge and its 18th century replacement, marking the boundary between Newcastle and Gateshead.

Four turrets, the highest a double-turret (above) to carry a flagpole, crown the roof of the Keep. The roof is 81ft from ground level. The height to the top of the flagpole turret is 100ft. However, these turrets and the battlements are not

The flagpole turret.

originals; they were added in the early 19th century.

Part of the curtain wall that surrounded the castle survives to the south, some of it behind the Bridge Hotel. A postern in this south wall leads to the Castle Stairs, which descend to the Close, Sandhill and Quayside. The remnants of a tower are also visible at the rear of the Bridge Hotel, close to the High Level Bridge. Other remains of the castle include those visible on its north eastern side, near Dog Leap Stairs.

Castle Stairs from the south.

The original main entrance to the castle was the Baillie or Bailiff Gate, on the south western side of the bailey and very close to the Keep. This entrance, also known as the Great Gate, has vanished.

The main entrance to the Castle Keep today.

A number of other buildings were erected in the bailey, including the Great Hall, stables and a kitchen. The Great Hall, now demolished, was next to the eastern curtain wall and is believed to have been built during the reign of John (1199-1216). It occupied the site of the present-day Vermont Hotel and part of the Moot Hall courtyard (see the map on page 77).

In 1292, the newly-crowned King of Scotland, John Baliol came to the Great Hall to do homage to Edward I of England. Edward was consolidating his claim to Scotland and his control of the man he had chosen to occupy the Scottish throne.

Accommodation for visiting monarchs was next to the Great Hall. This was probably because the Keep lacked the modern comforts demanded by royalty. King John, who spent much time in Newcastle, may have lodged in these royal apartments. Yet not all kings stayed in the castle as guests. Scotland's William the Lion and David II were briefly held prisoner there.

In 1247-1250, during the reign of Henry III, the Black Gate was built on the western side of the bailey to provide additional protection to the North Gate. A drawbridge and

This engraving of the Black Gate dates to around 1835. Shops and traders lined the narrow lane. It would become more of a slum than this picturesque view implies. Some of the houses were four storeys high, but only 10ft deep. The Black Gate itself accommodated twelve families and a public house.

ditch formed part of the defences.

The two upper storeys of the Black Gate were added on in the early 17th century. Further alterations, including a new roof, were made by the Society of Antiquaries of Newcastle upon Tyne in the 1880s.

Immediately behind the Black Gate passageway, within the castle grounds, are the remains of the Heron and Great pits, which were built as pits for an interior drawbridge. They were possibly later used as prison cells.

In 1400, Newcastle became a county in its own right, but the Castle Keep and Castle Garth (bailey), still under royal control, remained a part of Northumberland. A tiny part of

The Heron Pit (named after Keeper of the Castle William Heron, 1247-1258). Prisoners were reputedly dropped in from above by a trapdoor.

The Garrison Room in use as a prison. Conditions were appalling.

By the latter half of the 19th century the houses outside the Black Gate had been cleared. This photograph from St Nicholas Street was taken shortly before it was renovated by the Society of Antiquaries.

Northumberland therefore lay within Newcastle, and the Keep was used as the Northumberland county prison.

Iron rings, to which prisoners were chained as they awaited trial, can still be seen fixed to the wall of the Keep's Garrison Room.

The Great Hall in the Castle Garth was the courthouse. The

present Moot Hall, completed in 1812, replaced this earlier building and also serves as a courthouse.

The New Castle was less important as a defensive structure after the Town Walls were completed in the middle of the 14th century. The castle gradually decayed, and by the 16th century was described as 'ruinous'.

From the early 17th century onwards, the Castle Garth and Black Gate came under the control of a series of different leaseholders. The first of these was Alexander Stevenson, a page to James I. Sub-letting took place from that time onwards and many dwellings were built in the Garth.

The Black Gate is thought to have been named after Patrick Black, or his widow, Barbara, who succeeded Stevenson as leaseholder.

By the end of the 18th century, a warren of houses and shops occupied by traders in second-hand clothes, boots and shoes, crowded the grounds. The properties in the area immediately behind and in front of the Black Gate passageway were rented out to various traders in the same line of business. They lived in the rooms above their shops.

For some years the chapel in the Keep was used as a beer cellar for a public house and at one point a garden grew on top of its thick walls. Its roof had vanished.

In the early 19th century the Keep was acquired by Newcastle Corporation and rescued from dereliction. Four turrets, battlements and a new roof were created. In 1848 the Society of Antiquaries came to the rescue of the Castle Keep and the Black Gate and saved them from destruction by the building of the railway viaduct. They persuaded the Berwick and North Shields Railway to construct the viaduct between the buildings instead and the Society has preserved these historic structures ever since.

Eventually, most of the houses in the Castle Garth were cleared away, although the traders in clothes and shoes continued to occupy the Black Gate area for many years. Similar traders, mainly selling clogs, boots and shoes, occupied properties on the Castle Stairs.

This engraving dates to the early years of the 19th century, before the changes brought about by the coming of the railway. The battlements have been given crenellations, but the Keep seems to be being used as a dwelling to judge by the washing line and the wooden gate.

95

Today, the shopkeepers and houses have entirely disappeared, and the Black Gate is preserved. The Castle Keep is open to the public on a regular basis, enabling visitors and residents to tour the impressive stronghold that lies at the heart of Newcastle's extraordinary story.

The photograph above was taken in the early 1960s when the Black Gate, like most of Newcastle's buildings, was engrimed with soot. The gardens would be excavated in the 1970s to reveal the castle ditch, and Roman and Saxon remains.

Right, the Black Gate in 2011.